Auguste Mariette

The Monuments of Upper Egypt

Auguste Mariette

The Monuments of Upper Egypt

ISBN/EAN: 9783337323417

Printed in Europe, USA, Canada, Australia, Japan

Cover: Foto ©ninafisch / pixelio.de

More available books at **www.hansebooks.com**

THE MONUMENTS

OF

UPPER EGYPT

A TRANSLATION OF THE

"ITINÉRAIRE DE LA HAUTE ÉGYPTE"

OF

AUGUSTE MARIETTE-BEY

BY

ALPHONSE MARIETTE.

Non Jovis ira, nec ignes,
Nec poterit ferrum, nec edax abolere vetustas.
OVID.

ALEXANDRIA AND CAIRO: A. MOURÈS.
LONDON: TRÜBNER & Co.

1877.

THE TRANSLATOR'S PREFACE.

An unpretending little volume was published in 1869 under the title of *Itinéraire des Invités de S. A. le Khédive aux Fêtes de l'Inauguration du Canal de Suez.* The very title of the work is a record of the great historical event which gathered together many distinguished personages in Egypt.

The *Itinéraire* met with all the favour it deserved, and a first edition having been rapidly exhausted, a second one, with some slight alterations, appeared in 1872.

It soon became evident, however, that as the majority of regular tourists on the Nile belong to the two great English-speaking nations, an English edition of the *Itinéraire* would not prove otherwise than acceptable. At Mariette-Bey's request, being myself no stranger to Egypt, I readily undertook the required translation into English — a somewhat difficult task, in which

I was encouraged, however, by my brother's kindly expressed opinion that I would be all the better qualified for it by my genuine sympathy with the whole subject.

I have endeavoured to be faithful to the original text, keeping in view the author's idiosyncrasy, and I have but seldom thought fit to avail myself of the discretionary power that had been given me. My task, I need scarcely say, has been a pleasant one, and I shall feel amply repaid for the trouble incurred if I can but think that I have in the very remotest degree contributed to popularise Egypt's wonders, and to bring them and their English and American visitors into closer intercourse.

As stated in the second French edition, this little work does not pretend to replace Murray's *Handbook for Travellers in Egypt*, especially now that that excellent guide has been revised by a most competent writer. The aim of this volume is altogether different; it deals exclusively with the antiquities, and its sole object is to introduce the visitor to the Monuments of Upper Egypt, and to supply him with such information as will best enable him to understand their meaning.

In conclusion, I would take this opportunity of appealing earnestly to all travellers in Upper Egypt. For the sake of science, for the sake of those who will come after us—and I will add, in sheer justice to him whose persevering labours and truly heroic exertions have brought to light so many hidden treasures, I would entreat all visitors to Sakkárah, Abydos, Denderah, Thebes, etc., to watch with a jealous care over the integrity of monuments which no educated man can gaze upon without the keenest interest, and to prevent, as far as in their power lies, any further desecration of those relics of a glorious past.

ALPH. MARIETTE.

King's College, London,
May, 1877.

CONTENTS.

INTRODUCTION.

		PAGE
I.	SOURCES	1
	A Monuments	2
	The Temples	3
	The Tombs	6
	B Manetho	11
	C Classical Historians	12
II.	HISTORY	14
	1 Ancient Empire	15
	2 Middle Empire	16
	3 New Empire	16
	4 Lower Period	17
III.	CHRONOLOGY	18
	The Dynasties	22
IV.	RELIGION	23
V.	LANGUAGE AND WRITING	27
	Rosetta Stone	29
	Hieroglyphs	31
VI.	GENERALITIES	35
	A The decoration of the Temples	35
	B Their signification	38
	C The Mammisi	42
	D The Royal Cartouches	43
	E Epitome of the best-known epochs in Egyptian History	45
	F Entreaty to travellers to spare the Monuments	52
	G Papyrus to be carefully preserved	55

CONTENTS.

DESCRIPTION OF THE MONUMENTS .. 59

EXCURSIONS IN THE ENVIRONS OF CAIRO. 61

		PAGE
I.	HELIOPOLIS	61
II.	PYRAMIDS	65
	The three great Pyramids	67
	Their especial purpose	68
	The Sphinx	70
	The Great Pyramid	73
III.	MITRAHENNY	78
	Memphis	79
	Colossus of Rameses II.	85
IV.	SAḲḲÂRAH	86
	Necropolis	87
	Step-shaped Pyramid	87
	Serapeum	88
	Its discovery	89
	Tombs of Apis	90
	Tomb of Tih	94
	The mastabah, the serdab	95
	Scenes relating to the personage while still living	97
	Scenes relating to the death of the personage	99
	Scenes relating to the bringing in of funereal gifts	100
	Tomb of Phtah-Hotep	101

JOURNEY INTO UPPER EGYPT 105

I.	BENI HASSAN	106
	Pyramid of Meydoum	107
	Grotto tombs	109
	Tomb of Ameni-Amenemha	111
	Tomb of Noum-Hotep	112

CONTENTS.   xi

		PAGE
II.	ABYDOS	115
	Tel-Amarna	116
	Crocodile caves of Maabdeh	117
	Temple of Sethi I.	120
	Temple of Rameses II.	122
	Tablet of Abydos	122
	Kom-es-Sultan	123
III.	DENDERAH	125
	The Temple	126
	Divided into four groups	127
	1 Hypostyl Hall	127
	2 Chambers of Assembly	128
	Sacred barks	129
	Treasury, vestments, offerings	130
	3 Hypethral Temple	131
	4 Sanctuary	132
	The Crypts	135
	The Osiris of Denderah	137
	Hathor and her different attributes	141
IV.	THEBES	145
	Its history	147
	Its hieroglyphic name	153
	Its special divinity	155
	LUXOR	156
	Temple	156
	Sham antiquities	157
	KARNAK	157
	i. Temple of Khons	160
	Usurpation of authority by the Priests	160
	ii. The Great Temple	161
	Hypostyl Hall	162
	Bas-reliefs of Shishak	163
	Poem of Pen-ta-our	165
	Bas-reliefs of Sethi I.	166
	The Pylons	168
	The Obelisks	169
	The granite chambers	172

CONTENTS.

	PAGE
Geographical lists of Thothmes III.	174
Ethnological lists	175
Synoptical table of the Promised Land	176
Large court to the East	177
The Sanctuary	178
Hall of Ancestors	179
iii. The Ruins to the North	181
iv. The Ruins to the South	182
The Lake	182
The four Pylons	183
The Temple of Mout	185
THE TEMPLE OF GOORNAH	187
THE RAMESEUM	189
Episode in the life of Rameses II.	191
Gigantic statue of Rameses II.	194
THE COLOSSI	195
The Colossus of Memnon	197
Laudatory inscriptions	199
DEIR-EL-MEDINEH	200
MEDINET-ABOU	201
Temple of Thothmes III.	202
Temple of Rameses III.	203
A The Palace	204
Ethnological inscriptions	206
B The Temple	209
Battle scenes	210
Valuable inscription on pylon	212
More Battle scenes	214
Coronation and procession of Rameses III.	215
Naval battle	220
THE NECROPOLIS	222
Drah-abou'l-neggah	222
El-Assassif	223
Scheikh-abd-el-Goornah and Goornat-Mouraï	224
Tomb of Houï	225

CONTENTS. xiii

		PAGE
	Tomb of Petamenophis	227
DEIR-EL-BAHARI		228
	Triumphal entry of troops	230
BAB-EL-MOLOUK		233
	Tomb of Sethi I.	235
	Tomb of Rameses III.	239
	Tomb of Sethi II.	241
	Tomb of Rameses IV.	241
V. ESNEH		243
	Decadence of hieroglyphs	244
	Development of architecture	245
VI. EDFOU		246
	El Kab	246
	Temple of Edfou	247
	Name of architect	248
	The Sanctuary	249
	Dimensions	250
	Masts for pennants	251
VII. GEBEL-SILSILEH		251
	Stone quarries	252
	Speos	253
	Triumph of Horus	253
VIII. ASSOUÂN		254
	Ombos	254
	Mountains—Change of scenery	255
	Small temple	256
	Island of Elephantine	257
IX. PHILÆ		257
	Inscriptions on rocks	259
	Last resort of the Priests	260

MAP OF EGYPT TO THE FIRST CATARACT.
PLAN OF THE GREAT PYRAMID.
PLAN OF THE TEMPLE OF DENDERAH.
PLAN OF THE GREAT TEMPLE OF KARNAK.

LIST OF PUBLICATIONS RECOMMENDED.

Colonel Jacotin.—*Carte topographique de l'Egypte, levée pendant l'Expédition de l'Armée française.*

Linant de Bellefonds.—*Carte hydrographique de la Basse, de la Moyenne et de la Haute-Egypte.* Paris: Longuet.

Précis du système hiéroglyphique. Paris: Imprimerie Royale, 1828.

F. Champollion.—*Lettres écrites d'Egypte.* Paris: Didier.

——————. *Grammaire Egyptienne.* Paris: Didot.

Champollion-Figeac. — *L'Egypte ancienne (l'Univers Pittoresque).* Paris: Didot.

J. J. Ampère.—*Voyage et Recherches en Egypte et en Nubie.* Paris.

Sir Gardner Wilkinson.—*Manners and Customs of the Ancient Egyptians.* London, 1837 and 1841.

——————————. *Modern Egypt and Thebes.* London, 1843.

——————————. *The Egyptians in the Time of the Pharaohs,* with an Appendix by Dr. Birch, entitled *An Introduction to the Study of the Egyptian Hieroglyphs.* London, 1857.

E. W. Lane.—*An Account of the Manners and Customs of the Modern Egyptians.* London, 1871.

Bunsen.—*Egypt's Place in Universal History.*

H. Brugsch.—*Histoire d'Egypte;* 1ère partie, *L'Egypte sous les rois indigènes.* Leipzig: Hinrichs, 1859.

F. Lenormant.—*Manuel d'Histoire ancienne de l'Orient jusqu'aux Guerres médiques. Les Egyptiens,* tome I. Paris: A Lévy, 1869.

xvi PUBLICATIONS RECOMMENDED.

G. MASPERO.—*Histoire Ancienne des Peuples de l'Orient.* Paris: Hachette, 1875.

S. BIRCH.—*The Monumental History of Egypt.* London: S. Bagster.

Records of the Past, Vols. II., IV., and VI. London: S. Bagster.

MARIETTE-BEY.—*Aperçu de l' Histoire d'Egypte.* Cairo: A. Mourès, 1874.

——————. *Notice des Principaux Monuments du Musée de Boulaq.* Cairo: A. Mourès, 1876.

To the above should be added the other works of S. Birch, H. Brugsch and Mariette-Bey, as also the scientific publications on Egypt which bear the honoured names of Nestor L'Hôte, Ch. Lenormant, Hincks, Lepsius, E. de Rougé, de Saulcy, Goodwin and Chabas.

Many pleasant volumes of travels have been written on Egypt, or *à propos* of Egypt. We cannot enumerate them here; but we do not hesitate to single out, for its exceptional artistic and literary merit, *A Thousand Miles up the Nile*, by Amelia B. Edwards. London: Longmans, 1877.

THE

MONUMENTS OF UPPER EGYPT.

INTRODUCTION.

BEFORE embarking on the Nile the visitor should have mastered certain data which will afford a kind of preparation for the journey he is about to undertake. We will endeavour to supply, in as concise a form as possible, some of the requisite knowledge. We shall first treat of the sources from whence Egyptology, generally speaking, springs; we shall then refer successively to History, Chronology, and Religion, and after noticing Language and Writing, we will conclude by presenting together, in one chapter, under the head of Generalities, a few notes which could not well find a suitable place elsewhere.

I.—SOURCES.

All the monuments we are going to meet with belong to that civilisation which formerly flourished on the banks of the Nile, and which, from beginning to end, used hieroglyphs as its form of writing.

For the interpretation and understanding of those monuments Science avails herself of three different sources.

As a matter of course, the first and principal source is afforded by the monuments themselves, the undeniable witnesses, and often the contemporaries, of the events they relate. After them comes Manetho, an Egyptian priest, who wrote a history of Egypt in Greek; the third and last place being assigned to the Greek and Roman authors who travelled in Egypt, or who wrote about it from hearsay.

A.—MONUMENTS.

The monuments are at once many and various. Some are still in Egypt, some have found their way into the museums of various countries. As we have no intention of drawing up an inventory, be it ever so brief, of the monuments preserved in the Museums, we shall not go out of Egypt and will rest satisfied with supplying here a few *data* upon the temples and tombs, the only monuments the visitor to Upper Egypt will meet with on his way.*

1. **The Temples.**—This is not the right time to describe fully the temples one meets with while travelling in Upper Egypt, as such a description will be found presently in its appointed place. We may, however, put at once into the reader's hand the thread destined to guide him in the interior of those monuments.

A complete temple consists of the edifice properly so called, and an *enceinte* or surrounding wall. The temple is of stone, the outer wall is of large crude bricks, and is very high and very thick. When the entrance-gate is closed, nothing whatever can be heard or seen of what is taking place inside.

It would be a mistake to look at an Egyptian temple in the light of a church, or even of a Greek temple. Here no public worship is performed; the faithful do not congregate for public prayer; indeed, no one is admitted inside except the priests. The temple is a royal *proscynem*, or *ex voto*, that is, a token of piety from the king

* The ruins of cities are not included herein. The cities, properly so called, have completely disappeared, and their site is only here and there indicated by a few shapeless mounds.

who erected it in order to deserve the favour of the gods. It is a kind of royal oratory, and nothing more. In fact, this circumstance can alone explain the profuse decoration that covers the temples. Let the reader bear in mind that the principle of the decoration is the picture; that several pictures are ranged symmetrically side by side, and that several series of pictures, disposed in tiers one above the other, cover the walls of the chambers from top to bottom. Such is the invariable arrangement. As to the meaning of the pictures, it is everywhere the same. The king on one side and one or more divinities on the other—such is the sole subject of the composition. The king presents an offering (a table laden with victuals, flowers, fruit, and emblems) and solicits a favour from the god. In his answer, the god grants the gift that is prayed for. The decoration of the temple, therefore, consists of nothing more than an act of adoration from the king, repeated under every possible form. Thus a temple is the exclusively personal monument of the king by whom it was founded or decorated. Indeed, this accounts for the presence of those most invaluable battle-scenes with which the external walls of certain temples are adorned. It is to the god and to his protection that the king chiefly ascribes his victories. In fighting the enemies of Egypt, and in bringing them in chains into the temples, the king has done an act grateful to the gods, just as he has done an act grateful to the gods in offering to them incense, flowers, and the limbs of sacrificed animals. He therein gives proof of his piety and is all the more deserving of the favours which the construction of the temple is intended to secure.

The Egyptian temples are always dedicated to three gods. It is what Champollion calls the Triad. The first is the male principle, the second the female principle, and the third the offspring of the other two. But these three deities are blended into one. The father engenders himself in the womb of the mother and thus becomes at once his own father and his own son. Thereby are expressed the uncreatedness and the eternity of the Being who has had no beginning and who shall have no end.

The worship consists of prayers, recited within the temple in the name of the king, and above all, of processions. In these processions, which the king is supposed to head, are carried the insignia of the gods, the coffers in which their statues are enclosed, and also the sacred barks, which latter are generally deposited in the temple, to be brought out on fête days. In the middle, concealed under a veil, stands the coffer within which lies the emblem that none must see. The processions are commonly held within the temple; they generally ascend the terraces and sometimes spread themselves inside the inclosure away from the profane gaze, as we have already said. On rare occasions, the processions may be seen leaving the city and wending their way, either along the Nile or along a canal called the Sacred Canal, towards some other city more or less distant. Close to every temple is a lake. In all probability the lake played an important part in the processions, and the sacred barks were deposited there, at least while the fêtes lasted.

2. **The Tombs.** — The tombs are situated in the desert or in the side of a mountain more or less distant from the river. This accounts for their being relatively so well preserved. Less conspicuous than the houses of cities and the temples, they have been less exposed to devastations.

When complete a tomb consists of three parts.[*]

[*] We do not include in this description the tombs of the kings at Bab-el-Molouk, which are constructed on a different plan.

It is indicated from a distance by a small building rising in the necropolis — this is the first part. A rectangular and vertical well opens in some corner of the building and leads down into a vault—this is the second part. The third is the subterranean mausoleum, where the mummies repose.

The exterior building is not always solid. It sometimes contains one or several chambers, open at all times and to all comers, where the relatives of the defunct assemble with the offerings they have brought. There is also the *serdab*, that is, a kind of narrow passage left within the brickwork and walled in as soon as statues representing the defunct have been deposited inside. Of course this mysterious and inaccessible place remains for ever closed.*

The well presents no feature worthy of special attention. Its depth varies, as also its dimensions, according to the localities. Generally speaking, when once the mummy has been deposited in its place, the well is stopped up either

* When the tomb is hollowed out of the mountain, as at Beni-Hassan, it always consists of those three parts. The first chamber by which the tomb is entered takes the place of the exterior building. The well is in a corner of this chamber.

by a stone which hides its aperture, or by materials of all kinds heaped up there. Ropes are necessary for the descent.

The vault is cut into the rock, and so disposed that the sarcophagus is placed right under the principal chamber of the building, the one where the survivors assemble.

The traveller who visits the tombs of Saḳḳârah, of Beni-Hassan, of Goornah, and of El-Kab, must therefore understand that the chamber into which he will first enter, whether built of stone or whether hollowed in the rock, is the accessible chamber reserved for the relatives. The mummies are in a vault under ground, to which access is obtained by a narrow passage, which we call a well.

The decoration of the tombs is in accordance with certain laws, which vary according to the period or according to that part of the tomb which is to be ornamented. The well, the vault, and the *serdab*, are always without inscription. The stone sarcophagi and the wooden coffins of the mummies are often adorned with a vast amount of texts, interspersed with illustrations. All splendour of ornamentation was reserved for the chamber of the outer building.

It is not easy to point out the precise meaning of the decoration of the tombs of the Ancient Empire. The defunct is evidently at home. He fishes, he hunts; his servants bring him the products of his lands; dancing is held before him; his wife and children are by his side. But was it intended to represent the deceased as still of this world? And was it the object of the representations on the wall to preserve to us the remembrance of what he was during his lifetime? Or is he already in the other world, and, according to the somewhat naïve promises made to the Egyptians, will he continue in that other world to lead the same sort of life as he led here? We cannot discuss this question now. All we can say is that the promises of which we have just spoken are real: the defunct will some day live again in the plenitude of his faculties; he will have need of the same objects, he will occupy himself with the same interests; again will his family and servants be by his side. But never again will he suffer pain, nor be in apprehension of death. This seems to be the main idea which has presided at the decoration of the tombs under the Ancient Empire.

But a little later the decoration changes in its

character: the defunct must prove that he had gained this immortality which is promised him, and that by his merits he had deserved it.

The journey of the soul in the subterranean regions, the ordeals which it has to undergo, and its judgment, are the subjects which adorn the walls of the chambers in the exterior building. No more do we behold the varied scenes of hunting and fishing and of labour in the field. In their place appears the mournful procession of infernal deities.

At Sakkárah and at Beni-Hassan are found perfect examples of these chambers, where the defunct is represented as leading in the other world that domesticated and pastoral life which Egyptians regarded as the highest state of felicity.

It is at Bab-el-Molouk, in the tomb of Sethi I., that the type of the second sort of tomb is found.*

* For further details on this subject see the *Avant--propos* of the " Notice Sommaire des Monuments exposés dans les Galeries du Musée de Boulaq," which may be obtained at the museum at Boolák.

We have also treated of the tombs of the Ancient Empire, and the general idea on which their decoration rested, in a special article in the " Revue Archéologique " for January and February 1869. (Paris: Librairie Didier, Quai des Augustins.) See also S. Birch, " Unrolling of a Mummy."

B.—MANETHO.

Manetho was an Egyptian priest, who lived in the time of Ptolemy Philadelphus,* and who wrote a history of Egypt in Greek, in which he introduced a list of all the kings who ever reigned on the banks of the Nile, from the most remote period to the conquest of Alexander. This history is lost, but the lists are preserved in the work of Georgius Syncellus, a Byzantine historian of the eighth century, who had borrowed them from the *Chronicle* of Eusebius and from the *Chronography* of Julius Africanus.

After what we have already said, we need scarcely again refer to the lists of Manetho to point out of what importance they are for us. It may be that we cannot, strictly speaking, rely implicitly on the accuracy of the figures which mark the duration of the different reigns and dynasties, those figures having been rearranged by the Christian authors who copied them from the original work; and, moreover, it may be surmised that the names of some kings have been changed or inverted. Be that as it may, if for one moment we suppose the lists of Manetho had been entirely lost, through whom should we

* About the year 263 of the Christian era.

have become acquainted with that previous division into dynasties, and how should we even know that it ever existed? The royal names revealed by the hieroglyphic inscriptions become every day more and more numerous. How should we know in what manner to classify them at all satisfactorily without the lists of Manetho? Have not these lists the advantage—an advantage never sufficiently appreciated—of showing us at least a road which we may follow?

Among the sources of the history of Egypt, the Royal Papyrus of Turin, if it were complete, could alone rival Manetho in importance.

C.—CLASSICAL HISTORIANS.

Such persons as may not care to go deeply into the study of Egyptology may be content to read the Second Book of Herodotus, the First Book of Diodorus, the Seventeenth Book of Strabo, and the Treatise *de Iside et Osiride*, attributed to Plutarch.

Had we nothing but the writings of Herodotus and of Diodorus to guide us in the study of Ancient Egypt, we could certainly form but a very imperfect idea of that country. Every no-

tion of chronology is there completely upset.*
They contain stories as ridiculous as they are
impossible. One must read the histories of Egypt
written before the discovery of Champollion to
see into what fatal errors these two writers would
involve science, were no other sources of information at hand.

Strabo is more trustworthy. His *Geography*
contains excellent information, with no other
fault than that of being rather curtailed.

Whoever may have been the author of the
Treatise on Isis and Osiris, no one can enter
upon the study of the Egyptian religion without
an intimate acquaintance with this book. The
author has borrowed with discernment from true
Egyptian sources. In this world of ours, good
is incessantly struggling with evil, truth with
falsehood, light with darkness, life with death.
Osiris is one of the personifications of the eternal
antagonism of these two opposing principles. At
one moment overthrown by Typhon, the genius
of evil, Osiris dies; he revives only to fall
again. Out of this antagonism and the nu-

* Herodotus, for instance, places the Pyramids after
Rameses, which is very much like placing Charlemagne
after Louis XIV.

merous explanations and illustrations drawn from the myth the pseudo-Plutarch has woven the thread of his admirable *Treatise*.

II.—HISTORY.

The history of Egypt commences with Menes, the founder of the monarchy, and it terminates with the Emperor Theodosius, who abolished by a decree the ancient religion of the land (A.D. 381).

During this long period Egypt was not always mistress of her destinies. She had been conquered by the Shepherds, a horde of barbarians from Asia; by the Ethiopians, by the Greeks, and by the Romans, to say nothing of partial incursions of Libyan and Arabian tribes. But all these conquerors, not even excepting the Shepherds, adopted while in Egypt the religion, the arts, language, and customs of the conquered people; and their names figure in the official register of the kings of the country.

To establish some order in the endless list of kings who reigned from the time of Menes to that of Theodosius, one generally divides them, after Manetho's method, into royal families, or *Dynasties*, and these dynasties are in their turn distinguished from each other either by the name of the foreign nation which furnished the kings, or by the name of the city which served as capital in the time of such dynasty. Thus there is the Greek dynasty, the Memphite, the Theban, &c. From Menes to Theodosius there are as many as thirty-four different dynasties. Another and a wider division has been made. Taking into consideration certain important events and certain modifications introduced into the general economy of the kingdom, the entire history of Egypt has been divided into four main stems:—

1. The first comprises the first ten dynasties, and is called the *Ancient Empire*. The Ancient Empire belongs to a period so prodigiously remote that it is literally lost in the obscurity of ages. Its existence actually ceases before Abraham is born. The Ancient Empire spreads entirely over the fourth, the fifth, and part of the sixth dynasties. Before and after that, all is confusion, or rather darkness. This is the age of the Pyramids. It is a remarkable fact that the art of the statuary and of the sculptor reached a degree of perfection under the Ancient Empire which it was never again to attain.

2. The second extends over those centuries

that elapsed between the eleventh dynasty and the eighteenth. This is the *Middle Empire*. The Middle Empire has already been some time in existence when Abraham appears. Joseph is governor under the last king of the Middle Empire. Of the whole of this period, however, the twelfth dynasty and the Shepherd kings alone need be remembered. The twelfth dynasty is made famous by the tombs of Beni--Hassan. As to the Shepherds, or Hyksos, they give their name to the most lamentable period in Egyptian history, a period of 511 years, during which the national homogeneity is utterly broken, and Asiatic invaders lord it over the most flourishing provinces in the kingdom.

3. The third stem is that which is called the *New Empire*. It commences with the eighteenth dynasty and terminates with Alexander. The most brilliant epoch of the New Empire, that of which the most frequent and glorious traces are met with during a voyage on the Nile, corresponds to the eighteenth, nineteenth, and twentieth dynasties. It is the age of the Thothmes', the Amenophises, and the Rameses'. It is also the time of Moses (nineteenth dynasty). But this brilliancy was not to last, and when

Shishak (twenty-second dynasty) took Jerusalem, the decline of Egypt had already begun.

4. The fourth stem, to which the general name of *Lower Period* is given, includes the Greek dynasty founded by Alexander and that of the Roman emperors, who were kings of Egypt by the same right as Cambyses and Darius. The history of this epoch, entirely taken up as it is with a fruitless competition for the throne, possesses but a feeble interest. The traveller in Upper Egypt, however, should not pass it by because the temples of Philæ, of Edfou, of Ombos, of Denderah, and of Esneh, that is to say, the most complete monuments which we possess of Egyptian worship, belong to the Lower Period.

A primary division of the kings of Egypt into Dynasties, according to the type furnished by Manetho, and a further division of the dynasties into *Ancient Empire*, *Middle Empire*, *New Empire*, and *Lower Period*, such, then, is the starting-point of all study of Egyptian history, and consequently the starting-point of the classification of all the temples the tourist will meet with in his journey on the Nile.

It is evident that a history of Egypt would

here be well placed, and would be the very best preparation for the voyage. But we could not possibly, without exceeding our limits, place under the eyes of the reader, were it ever so briefly, an account of those events which procured for Egypt so wide an influence over the destinies of the ancient world.

A few years since we prepared for the use of the Egyptian schools a small "Aperçu de l'Histoire d'Egypte." Those who do not care to go very deeply into the subject, or who would be satisfied with general views, may make themselves acquainted with its pages. If more details be desired, penned by a competent hand, let the *History* of M. Brugsch be consulted.*

III.—CHRONOLOGY.

Egypt is surpassed by no other nation in point of antiquity. Prehistoric remains, it is true, carry us back to a much more remote period,

* "Histoire d'Egypte dès les premiers temps de son existence jusqu'à nos jours," part i.. comprising "L'Egypte sous les rois indigènes" (Hinrichs, Leipsic, 1859). See also M. François Lenormant's *résumé* in his "Manuel d'Histoire ancienne de l'Orient," vol. i., p. 828 and following (A. Lévy, Paris, 1869).

but if we seek monuments that bear the stamp of an already refined civilisation, the most ancient are certainly to be found in Egypt.

But easy as it may be to believe in the tradition which assigns to Egypt so prodigious an antiquity, it is equally difficult to bring forward scientific proofs of that antiquity. Records of eclipses and other astronomical phenomena, which are still wanting, could alone furnish the required testimony.

In the meantime, we have no other source but the lists of Manetho and the dates inscribed in these lists. Unfortunately, disorder reigns supreme here. Not only the dates taken from Manetho are not in accordance with extracts taken from Julius Africanus and Eusebius, but we possess two versions of the *Chronicle* of Eusebius the dates of which do not agree with each other. On the other hand, it too often happens that the hieroglyphs themselves furnish us with dates which contradict the duration assigned to certain reigns by the national historian. It will be easily understood, therefore, to how much error we are exposed when we wish, for example, to fix the date of the foundation of the Egyptian monarchy.

And yet, for all that, it must be admitted that the authority of Manetho, an Egyptian priest, writing the history of his own country from the archives of the temples, should always carry great weight. In vain is it alleged that several of the dynasties which he cites as successive were contemporaneous. If the fact were proved, we must evidently deduct from the total amount the entire duration of those dynasties which have thus grafted themselves, like so many branches, upon the main stem. But the system of contemporaneous dynasties is as yet supported by no really trustworthy proof; on the contrary, it seems certain that Manetho was well aware that at various epochs Egypt was governed simultaneously by several dynasties, and he availed himself of the means of control at his disposal to strike out of his work all such dynasties as did not belong to the genuine series of royal houses who succeeded each other on the throne, so that the latter were alone officially enrolled in due order on the register of kings. It is true, Manetho's figures have undoubtedly suffered serious alterations. But if we consider that they have come down to us through Christian writers, who had an evident interest in curtailing them, we shall see that, as a matter of fact, far from ascribing too wide a range to those figures, we are bound, as fair critics, to accept them as having been systematically reduced in their total amount.

The authority, then, of Manetho as a chronologist remains unshaken, but on condition that we only take the dates which he gives us as approximate. Certain as it is that those dates are not absolutely exact, yet it is difficult to believe that they have been so radically altered as not in any degree to come near to the truth. Anyhow, the nearer we approach the source of those alterations, the more we shall feel compelled to admit that if the lists could have reached us intact from the hand of Manetho, we would find them extending over a still wider range of time.

From these remarks it will be understood that the following table of Egyptian dynasties is presented to the reader under all reserve; and it is almost superfluous to add that the simultaneous dynasties are not included here; that the dynasties are presented in the same order as in Manetho; and, moreover, that the dates are, with one or two exceptions, the same as those given by the national historian :—

THE MONUMENTS OF UPPER EGYPT.

	Number of Dynasty.	Name of Dynasty.	Duration.	Date B.C.
ANCIENT EMPIRE.	I.	Thinite	253 years	5004
	II.	Thinite	302 ,,	4751
	III.	Memphite	214 ,,	4449
	IV.	Memphite	284 ,,	4235
	V.	Memphite	248 ,,	3951
	VI.	Elephantine	203 ,,	3703
	VII.	Memphite	70 days	—
	VIII.	Memphite	142 years	3500
	IX.	Heracleopolite	109 ,,	3358
	X.	Heracleopolite	185 ,,	3249
MIDDLE EMPIRE	XI.	Theban	213 ,,	3064
	XII.	Theban		
	XIII.	Theban	453 ,,	2851
	XIV.	Xoite	184 ,,	2398
	XV.	Shepherds		
	XVI.	Shepherds	511 ,,	2214
	XVII.	Shepherds		
NEW EMPIRE.	XVIII.	Theban	241 ,,	1703
	XIX.	Theban	174 ,,	1462
	XX.	Theban	178 ,,	1288
	XXI.	Tanite	130 ,,	1110
	XXII.	Bubastite	170 ,,	980
	XXIII.	Tanite	89 ,,	810
	XXIV.	Saite	6 ,,	721
	XXV.	Ethiopian	50 ,,	715
	XXVI.	Saite	138 ,,	665
	XXVII.	Persian	121 ,,	527
	XXVIII.	Saite	7 ,,	406
	XXIX.	Mendesian	21 ,,	399
	XXX.	Sebennyte	38 ,,	378
	XXXI.	Persian	8 ,,	340
LOWER PERIOD.	XXXII.	Macedonian	27 ,,	332
	XXXIII.	Greek	275 ,,	305
	XXXIV.	Roman	411 ,,	30

IV.—RELIGION.

Jamblichus, a writer who lived at the end of the third century, represents the Egyptians as believing in one God, unique, universal, uncreate—the Author of his own being, having no beginning, existing from eternity. Jamblichus goes on to say that under this supreme deity are a number of other gods who personify his divine attributes. Thus Ammon is that hidden force in nature which brings all things into life.

The supreme intellect, in which all other intellects are summed up, is Imothis. Phtah is the creative essence, which accomplishes all things with perfection and with truth. Osiris is the good and beneficent deity. If Jamblichus is a faithful recorder of Egyptian traditions, his statements would imply that, though degenerated by a belief in inferior gods personifying the qualities of the Supreme Being, a peculiar monotheism was once the foundation of the Egyptian religion.

The monuments themselves give us some glimpses of this belief. At Tell-Amarna, Aten is often styled the One God. At Thebes and at Memphis, Ammon and Phtah are clothed with the attributes of the Supreme Deity. Ammon is father to himself; he is the generating spirit from the very commencement, the twofold Being, at once father and mother, and existing from all eternity.

On this foundation rests the whole edifice of the Egyptian religion. To the initiated of the sanctuary, no doubt, was reserved the knowledge of the god in the abstract, the god concealed in the unfathomable depths of his divine essence. But for the less refined adoration of the people who required, so to speak, a palpable and a tangible god, were presented the images of the divinities sculptured on the walls of the temples. Such are the ideas which thus far have been accepted by the scientific world, and the only classical authority on which the whole tradition rests is the passage in Jamblichus.

Unfortunately, the more one studies the Egyptian religion, the greater becomes the doubt as to the character which must definitively be ascribed to it. A most fertile source of materials has recently been placed at our disposal by the excavations of the temples of Denderah and of Edfou. From one end to another, these temples are covered with legends, and present every appearance of being two books which treat, *ex professo*, of religion generally and more particularly of the gods to whom these temples are dedicated. But neither in these temples nor in those which were previously known to us does the one god of Jamblichus appear. If Ammon at Thebes is the "first of the first," if Phtah at Memphis is the father of all creation, without beginning and without end, it is because all the Egyptian gods are in turn clothed with the attributes of the Eternal. In other terms, we find everywhere deities who are immortal and uncreated; but nowhere do we find the One and invisible God, without name and without form, who presides from on high over the Egyptian Pantheon. Thus no indication to that effect is given by the temple of Denderah, the most hidden inscriptions of which have now been thoroughly examined. What we may rather gather from the study of this temple is that, with the Egyptians, the universe itself was God, and that Pantheism formed the basis of their religion. We should, therefore, feel disposed to modify, in favour of this view, the general ideas which we have expressed in the "Notice du Musée" (fourth edition, p. 20). "The theology of the Egyptians, from whom Orpheus borrowed his ideas," says Eusebius in his *Evangelical Preparation*, "acknowledged that the universe is God, composed of several divinities which constitute his different parts." The passage in Jamblichus must, then, give way, as a classical authority, to the passage in Eusebius.

However this may be, and in whatever light we are to consider the Egyptian divinities, an equal amount of worship was not paid to these divinities in all parts of Egypt. Ammon was adored at Thebes, Phtah at Memphis, Cnouphis at Elephantine, Horus at Edfou, Hathor at Denderah, Neith at Saïs, Soutekh at Tanis. Thus Egypt was divided, religiously as well as geographically, into districts each of which possessed its local worship, and the gods thus shared among themselves the religious government of the country. An exception, however, was made in favour of Osiris. The presiding deity of the abode of departed spirits, Osiris, was the god universally worshipped, and was equally venerated in all parts of Egypt.

V.—LANGUAGE AND WRITING.

The Egyptian language is neither Semitic nor Indo-European. It is one of the principal types of that group of languages which may be called Chamitic. The Coptic language is this same Egyptian language as it was spoken in the second or third century of our era, when it was used to express Christian ideas.*

There are still many persons who firmly believe that hieroglyphs are nothing but a series of riddles which, when taken collectively, form a sort of enigma to be guessed at, and it must be confessed that this error is encouraged by the most serious classical writers: "The right hand open, with extended fingers," says Diodorus Siculus, "represents the desire of acquisition; the left hand closed, the grasping and keeping of property."

"To express hatred," says Plutarch, "they depict a fish. At Saïs, in the vestibule of the temple of Minerva, there were engraved a child, an old man, a hawk, a fish, and a hippopo-

* One should bear in mind that when the Egyptian language became merged into Coptic it had already greatly degenerated, so that the Coptic language represents the language of the demotic character rather than that of the hieroglyphs.

tamus. Evidently these were so many symbols which meant: 'Oh, ye who are entering upon life, and ye who are ready to quit it, God hates impudence, arrogance, pride of heart, and self-sufficiency.' Thus the entrance into life is expressed by a child, death by an old man, divinity by a hawk, hatred by a fish, because of the sea, and impudence by the hippopotamus."—"A vulture signifies nature," says Ammianus Marcellinus. "Why? Because it is said that amongst those creatures no males are to be found. A king is symbolised by a bee making honey. Why? Because the king is the director of his people, whom he ought to be able to check by his gentleness, at the same time that he incites them."*

The discovery of Champollion, however, has

* These traditions are not entirely without foundation. A *fish* is pronounced *betu*, and *betu* means *evil, sin, abomination*. The *bee* is pronounced *sekhet*, and designates the sovereignty over Lower Egypt. If the temple of Minerva at Saïs belonged to the Lower Period, it may well be that, in accordance with the *manière* spirit of the times, and regardless of all grammatical connection, they wrote a *child*, an *old man*, a *hawk*, a *fish*, a *hippopotamus*, for what would thus be rendered, "Oh, child, oh, old man, the divinity holds all evil in abomination" (the hippopotamus being considered as a typhonian animal). Strictly speaking, therefore, Diodorus, Plutarch and Ammianus Marcellinus do not lead us into absolute error. But

dispelled these errors. Hieroglyphic writing is not enigmatical; it is read and pronounced just as Hebrew or Syriac is pronounced, and possesses an alphabet of its own.

The chief instrument of the success of Champollion's discovery is the monument known throughout the world as the *Rosetta Stone*.

The Rosetta Stone is a fragment of a stela * discovered in the year 1799 by M. Boussard,

what is false is at once the point from whence they start and the conclusion at which they arrive. Because the Egyptians once made a play upon words with *child, old man*, &c., it does not follow that this sort of riddle should be the universal rule of all hieroglyphic writing. The authors we have been quoting seem to have had no idea that hieroglyphic writing could be alphabetic, and they have helped to keep up this error until the present time.

* This is one of the words most frequently used in Egyptian archæology, because it designates a monument which is found in hundreds. The stela is a rectangular flat stone generally rounded at the summit, and it was made use of by the Egyptians for all sorts of inscriptions. These stelæ were, generally speaking, used for epitaphs; they also served, however, to transcribe texts which were to be preserved or exhibited to the public, and in this latter case the stela became a sort of monumental placard. In addition to the Rosetta Stone, which is in the British Museum, the following are reckoned among the most celebrated stelæ, viz. the Stone of Sân, the Stone of Cheops, the Tablet of Alexander II., the five Tablets of Gebel-Barkal, and the Stela of Thothmes III., all of which belong to the Museum at Boolâk.

a French artillery officer, while digging entrenchments round the town of that name. It contains a copy of a decree made by the priests of Egypt, assembled at Memphis, in honour of Ptolemy Epiphanes. This decree is engraved on the stone in three languages, or rather in three different writings. The first is the hieroglyphic, the grand old writing of the monuments; the second is the demotic character as used by the people; and the third is the Greek. But the text in Greek character is the translation of the two former. Up to this time, hieroglyphs had remained an impenetrable mystery even for science. But a corner of the veil was about to be lifted: in proceeding from the known to the unknown, the sense at all events was at length to be arrived at of that mysterious writing which had so long defied all the efforts of science. Many erudite scholars tried to solve the mystery, and Young, among others, very nearly brought his researches to a satisfactory issue. But it was Champollion's happy lot to succeed in entirely tearing away the veil.

Such is the Rosetta Stone, which thus became the instrument of one of the greatest discoveries which do honour to the nineteenth century.

Thanks to this discovery, we are now in a position to affirm that hieroglyphic writing is not an idle play upon words. It is scarcely more complex or more difficult to read than any other writing. When once one can accustom oneself to see an *a* in an eagle, 🦅, a *b* in a human leg, ⌓, a *c* in a bolt, ⎯, and so forth, the difficulties are soon overcome. What has for so many centuries distracted attention from the true meaning of the hieroglyphics is the somewhat singular selection of the forms adopted to represent the letters of the alphabet. *A priori*, it was natural to imagine that this singular medley of representations of animals and of ordinary objects could only be taken figuratively; and as a certain halo of mystery had always enshrouded all things pertaining to Ancient Egypt, it was quite natural to believe that under these symbols the priests concealed their religious mysteries. But now the veil has been rent asunder, and hieroglyphic writing has become not much more difficult to decipher than any other Eastern character.

In consequence of the nature of the signs of which hieroglyphic writing is composed, it can be written either in vertical or in horizontal lines. In examining a hieroglyphic text, it will be easily observed that all the heads of animals or of men are turned in the same direction. It is from that side towards which the heads are turned that the inscription begins. Consequently, according to the desire of the scribe, the hieroglyphs could be disposed in such a manner as to be read either from left to right, or from right to left.*

In a hieroglyphic inscription there are some signs which should be pronounced and some which should not be pronounced. The former are much the most numerous. They include in the first place such signs as are purely alphabetical. The alphabet itself contains twenty-four letters; but there are several different forms for the *a*, several for the *b*, &c. &c. In the second place they include syllabic signs: thus a chessboard, ▬, has a pronunciation of

* The hieratic and demotic characters are more rapid writings derived in different degrees from the hieroglyphs themselves. They are scarcely ever employed except for the papyri. One finds, however, at Gebel-Silsilch some excellent specimens of the former of these characters; and at Philæ are to be found engraved on the walls of the temple a considerable number of *proscynems*, or *ex votos*, in the demotic character.

its own, *men*; an upright vase, ⟨vase⟩, is pronounced *hes*; the plant. ⟨plant⟩. has the sound of *mes*, &c. In the third place, they include the ideal sounds: a lion is represented by a *lion*, a horse by a *horse*, &c. And in the fourth place they include symbolic signs, that is to say, such as are diverted from their true meaning in order to symbolise an idea; thus the vulture, ⟨vulture⟩, signifies *mother*, the cubit, ⟨cubit⟩, represents *justice*, &c.

The signs not to be pronounced are the expletives, which are used to call the attention of the reader to the text or to the meaning of the word they accompany. Nor are the very numerous signs which Champollion has called *determinatives*, to be pronounced either. Thus, after all names of quadrupeds, the scribe draws the sign ⟨tail⟩, which represents *the tail of a quadruped;* all such words as refer to speech, to thought, to affection, or anything expressing an emotion of the soul, are sometimes followed by the figure of *a man putting his hand to his mouth,* ⟨man⟩; *a man in a crouching position raising one arm,* ⟨crouching man⟩, determines proper nouns, &c., &c. The crouching man, the man placing his hand on his mouth, and the tail of the quadruped are signs which are not pronounced; but the presence of these signs points out that the word which precedes them is either a proper noun or a word expressing a sentiment, or the name of a quadruped, &c. &c.

Such, then, is the construction of hieroglyphic writing in its principal features. At first sight it seems complicated; but in reality the use of the determinatives affords great help, and, however obscure or mysterious a hieroglyphic text may appear, it is certainly by no means more difficult to decipher than a Hebrew text, nor does its translation require so great an effort of mind as that of a passage of Chinese.

We must not forget to add that the task of interpreting hieroglyphic texts is facilitated by the fact that the Coptic tongue is derived from the language which lies hidden under the ancient Egyptian writing. And this Coptic tongue, whose connection with the old language can easily be traced, has a vocabulary and a grammar well known to scholars, and, although justly reckoned among the dead languages, it continues to live in its literature.

VI.—GENERALITIES.

A.—The decoration of the temples demands some explanations. The reader knows already that that decoration consists of sculptured pictures, and that these pictures are arranged side by side and in several rows one above the other, in such a manner as to cover symmetrically from top to bottom the walls of the chambers. The reader is also aware that all the pictures are composed on a uniform plan. The king is on one side, the divinity on the other, and the texts accompanying these pictures are also drawn up on one and the same plan: on the side of the king, his names and a few titles in accordance with the offerings made, and then the words which the king is supposed to pronounce; on the side of the divinity, his name and titles, and an answer wherein gifts are conceded proportionate with the offering. To give a general idea of these pictures as to disposition and style, we will select for description the whole lower row of one of the walls of the corridor R, in the temple of Denderah.*

* On the north side of the corridor, the lower register to the left on entering.

1st picture.—The king offers to the goddess Hathor the vase which serves in hieroglyphics to designate the word *heart*. In token of her satisfaction, the goddess promises to the king all kinds of happiness and joy.

2nd picture.—Hathor and Horus of Edfou are standing up at one end of the picture. At the other end, the king makes an offering of the two *sistra*, emblems which in this temple represent more particularly evil overcome, and consequently happiness. "Mayest thou be loved by women," replies Hathor, alluding to that sistrum which signifies happiness; "mayest thou find favour with their lords." Horus, on his side, responds to the offering of the other sistrum: "May Egypt conduct herself as thou wouldst have her; mayest thou tread under foot all foreign countries."

3rd picture.—The king offers incense and a libation to Osiris-Onnophris and to Isis, "to fill their divine nostrils with the perfumes of incense, and to refresh their hearts with the waters of the renovated Nile." In return, Osiris promises the king a favourable inundation, while Isis vouchsafes to him a long dominion over Arabia and the other countries which produce incense.

4th picture.—The king offers two vases full of wine to Hathor and to a god who seems to be Horus. Hathor promises him those regions which produce the best grapes, namely, *Kenemen, T"est'es*, and *Neham*. Horus promises him wine to satiety.

5th picture.—At the same time that he offers her flowers, the king addresses himself in the following terms to Hathor : " I bring thee bouquets of flowers of all kinds, that thou mayest adorn thy head with their colours." In her answer, the goddess promises the king that under his reign the land shall be made merry with the most brilliant verdure.

6th picture.—An offering of the hieroglyph which expresses fields is made to Hathor and to her son Hor-sam-ta-ui. The god Ahi, a duplicate of the person of the king, considered as the third person of the triad, stands before Hathor. The gifts bestowed on the king consist of corn in immense quantities, and of cereals of all kinds.

7th picture.—The king and the queen offer the two sistra to Isis and to Ahi, to solicit the favour of these divinities. Isis grants to the king the love of his subjects.

8th picture.—The king is in the presence of Isis and of Hor-sam-ta-ui. He makes a general offering of food, of flowers, of fruit, and of bread. Isis replies: "I give thee everything in the heavens, all that the earth produces, and everything that the Nile can bring." Hor-sam-ta-ui replies: "I give thee all that emanates from the rays of the sun, to fill thy dwelling with victuals."

The above is a fair specimen of the pictures that form the decoration of an Egyptian temple, and which the visitor may invariably expect to meet with on entering. These pictures always consist of an offering on the one side, and a gift bestowed on the other, the whole being expressed by a sort of dialogue between the personages represented.

B.—In visiting an Egyptian temple one soon becomes accustomed to see in the various chambers, and in the sculptures that adorn them, the chapters and pages of a single book, conceived with a unity of idea which develops itself on the walls of the temple from the entrance gate to the depths of the sanctuary. The king is in adoration, and throughout this act of adoration he develops an idea common to the entire temple: such is the basis of the decoration of the monument.

In the temples of Pharaonic origin (Karnak, Luxor, Medinet-Abou, Abydos, &c.) this rule does not generally hold good. The decoration is vague. The king adores the divinity of the place, but there is no reason why the picture should be in one part rather than in another; indeed, one finds, at the entrance of the temple, pictures which might just as well have been placed at the far end, without their meaning being in the least affected.*

But temples of Ptolemaic origin are more precise. Their composition is more scientific. The decoration of each chamber is in accordance with its purpose. The two chambers which at Edfou

* The six vaulted chambers of the grand temple of Abydos are an exception to this rule. All the pictures relate to ceremonies which the king ought successively to perform. The king, presenting himself on the right side of the door, proceeded all round the hall, and departed at the left side. Statues were disposed around the chamber. The king opened the door of the *naos*, or shrine, in which they were inclosed, and as soon as he perceived the statue he offered it incense, and, lifting the vestment which covered it, he laid his hands upon it, and perfumed t, and then replaced the draperies, &c.

and at Denderah are called the treasury of the temple* can be studied in reference to this subject. The king presents himself at the entrance of the chamber, holding in his hand a coffer in which are inclosed ingots of gold and silver, and precious stones. In the interior he is represented as offering to the divinity necklaces, sistra, head-dresses enriched with precious stones, mirrors, and sceptres. In the other chambers,† which are the laboratories of the temple, the king offers the sacred oils, essences, and aromatics which are there prepared, and which serve either to perfume the temple or to anoint the statues of the gods. Now and then, though unfortunately but seldom, we even find, divided into several sections, the various successive scenes of a common action. On entering the temple of Denderah by the magnificent hall of twenty-four columns, we find immediately on the right four pictures which are worthy of attention. Before penetrating into the most holy place the king must submit to a certain initiation. In the first picture, he has his sandals on

* See hall J in the subjoined plan of the temple of Denderah.
† See hall F in the plan of the temple of Denderah.

his feet and his staff in his hand. He enters the temple preceded by five banners, which probably accompany him along the whole route. The next picture shows us the scene of purification. The king is purified by the flood of water which Thoth and Horus are supposed to pour over him under the form of a double jet of the emblems of life. In the third picture, the king receives the two crowns which denote his sovereignty over Egypt, from the hands of the goddess of the South and the goddess of the North. Thus crowned, the king is admitted into the presence of Hathor, conducted on one side by Mout of Thebes, and on the other by Toum of Heliopolis. He advances to enjoy the felicity of contemplating the divine majesty. In return, the goddess promises him "annals written for eternity," *i.e.* an everlasting glory.*
This forms the subject of the fourth picture. Episodes no less interesting are represented at Edfou in the two first halls. The king leaves

---

* On entering the first hall of the temple of Edfou one perceives on the right hand and on the left two small edifices let into the wall between the columns of the façade. That on the right is the library; the one on the left is the little chamber where the king underwent the ceremonies of purification.

his palace and comes to lay the first stone of the temple. He fashions a brick with his own hands; he traces on the ground the furrow which shall mark the area of the temple. He lays a foundation-stone. He performs the ceremony of the presentation of the temple to the god in whose honour it has been erected. On this occasion he decapitates a bird, &c.*

But, apart from these episodes, it is difficult at first sight to discover the idea which has presided at the decoration of a chamber. This idea can eventually be realised in temples of Ptolemaic origin (Denderah, Edfou, Thebes, &c.), but we would look for it in vain elsewhere.

C.—By the side of many temples of Ptolemaic epoch may be seen smaller edifices, remarkable for the monstrous forms which decorate the capitals of the columns, and which are also used as ornaments in various parts of the interior. The authors of the great work of the "Commission d'Egypte" gave to these temples the name of *Typhonium*. Champollion called them *Mammisi*. According to Champollion,

* For similar scenes see the lower register on the right-hand side on entering the hall B of the temple of Denderah.

"these Mammisi were always constructed by the side of the larger temples where a triad was worshipped, and they represented the celestial abode where the goddess had given birth to the third person of the triad."

It must be observed that the monstrous forms of which we have just been speaking have nothing to do with Typhon, the god of evil, and the eternal enemy of Osiris. The god thus represented is called *Bes* in the Egyptian language. Far from presiding over evil, he is the god who symbolises mirth and dancing, and it is on that account that he so often appears on articles of the toilette-table. As such also his image is sculptured on the walls of the *Mammisi*. One sees by this how unsuitable is the appellation of *Typhonium*. The *Typhonia* spoken of by Strabo in reference to Denderah were more likely to be the various parts of the desert appropriated to the necropolis.

D.—It is impossible to travel in Upper Egypt without knowing what is meant by a *cartouche*. A cartouche is that elongated oval terminated by a straight line which is to be seen on every wall of the Egyptian temples, and of which other monuments also afford us numerous examples. The cartouche always contains the name of a king or of a queen, or in some cases the names of royal princesses.* To designate a king there are most frequently two cartouches side by side. The first is called the *prenomen*, the second the *nomen*. The prenomen-cartouche is usually preceded by the titles of *King of Upper and Lower Egypt*, and the nomen-cartouche by the title of *Son of the Sun*, represented thus :—

They are sometimes replaced by other titles, in this way :—

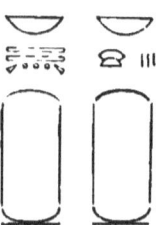

---

* It is sometimes found, as for instance at Denderah, applied to the names of gods, in which case the gods are considered as dynastic.

which when interpreted mean : *Lord over the two worlds, Lord of crowns.*

Most frequently the cartouches rest on their base in an upright position; there is nothing, however, in the structure of the Egyptian writing that prevents their being placed horizontally, as in this example :—

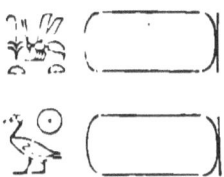

In visiting a temple the cartouches should always be carefully studied, as they fix the date of the monument.

E.—The cartouches known up to the present time are very numerous, but for a journey into Upper Egypt it is not necessary to be acquainted with all of them. At the risk of some repetition, we will enumerate the epochs and names which will be most frequently met with by the traveller in those regions.

During an excursion into Upper Egypt we find no traces of the three first dynasties, unless, perhaps, it be the step-shaped Pyramid of Sakkárah. The Great Pyramids (those of Cheops, Chephren and Mycerinus) belong to the IVth dynasty. The tombs of Tih and Phtah-hotep, and all the tombs which are visited at Sakkárah belong to the Vth. To find records of the VIth, the traveller must visit some less frequented spots, such as Zawyet-el-Maïtin, Qasr-es-sayad, and the El-Kab rocks. The necropolis of Abydos has supplied the Museum at Boolâk with some valuable stelæ of the VIth dynasty.

The VIIth, VIIIth, IXth and X[th] dynasties are a complete blank. There is no monument known which can be assigned to this period with any degree of certainty.

The XIth dynasty is a revival. Thebes then becomes a capital for the first time; and the tombs of this XIth dynasty are found in that part of the necropolis of Thebes which is called Drah-abou'l-neggah.

The XIIth dynasty is represented by the tombs of Beni-Hassan, and the names of its kings often occur in the necropolis of Abydos. During the excavations made at Karnak, we have discovered many fragments of statues and of tables of offerings belonging to this period.

The XIIIth and XIVth dynasties have left but few traces. Scarcely any cartouches of the kings of this period figure on the scarabœi and statues found in the necropolis of Abydos. Near Assouân, and in the isle of Sehel (first Cataract) the names of some kings of the XIIIth dynasty are sculptured on the rocks.

The next three dynasties are taken up by the Shepherd Kings. Another great blank occurs here in the monumental history. The national life is extinguished. We only find traces of the Shepherds in Lower Egypt, and more particularly at San (the Tanis of the Bible).

In Thebes alone are concentrated the XVIIIth, XIXth and XXth dynasties. Egypt revives after the expulsion of the Shepherds, and civilisation takes a considerable start. Karnak is enlarged; Deir-el-Bahari is built, together with Luxor, the temple of Goornah, the Rameseum and Medinet--Abou. In the Valley of the West, and at Bab--el-Molouk, vaults are excavated which are destined to serve as tombs to the kings of these three dynasties.

The XXIst dynasty was twofold. At Thebes the high priests of Ammon usurped the power, and had themselves proclaimed kings. They finished the temple of Khons. During this time the legitimate dynasty reigned at Tanis, and under its sway some additions were made to the temple of that city.

Of the XXIInd and the three following dynasties we find but few monumental traces. This period is marked by severe struggles in the north and in the south. The wall called the Wall of the Bubastites at Karnak dates from the XXIInd dynasty. A part of the southernmost wall of Karnak and a small temple built on the north side, at the very foot of the inclosing wall, bear the names of Sabacon and Tahraka, Ethiopian kings of the XXVth dynasty.

The XXVIth dynasty (the third renaissance) occupied itself but little with Upper Egypt. Its seat of government was Saïs. Names of some of its kings, however, are to be found on the leaning column of the great hall at Karnak and on the large columns at Luxor.

The XXVIIth dynasty belongs to the Persians. The XXVIIIth, XXIXth and XXXth correspond to an anxious period, during which Egypt, naturally kept uneasy by the presence of the Persians, had other things to think of than the erection of monuments.

The Persians have left some souvenirs on the rocks of the valley of Hamamât, near Keneh. One finds here and there traces of Achoris and of Nepherites on the walls of Medinet-Abou, and in the subterranean tombs of Abd-el--Goornah; and to Nectanebo II. we owe the most ancient constructions in the isle of Philæ.

The XXXIst dynasty again belongs to the Persians. Darius was then king; he was overthrown by Alexander, who commenced the XXXIInd dynasty. His son, Alexander II., constructed the portal the uprights of which are still standing at Elephantine. The granite sanctuary at Karnak was restored by Philip.

Next come the Ptolemies. Philadelphus (Ptolemy II.) builds an important portion of Philæ, and he appropriates to his own cartouches some spaces left unoccupied by his predecessors on the vast monumental walls of Karnak. Euergetes I. (Ptolemy III.) raised in front of the temple of Khons at Thebes the magnificent gateway which corresponds to the other portal situated to the north, and which was also erected by this prince. Philopator (Ptolemy IV.) founded on the left bank of the Nile the pretty little temple of Deir-el-Medineh, and he also commenced the admirable edifice of Edfou. At Philæ are found the cartouches of Epiphanes (Ptolemy V.), as well as those of Philometor (Ptolemy VI.) who again appears at Karnak, and whose name is also found at the end of the hypostyle hall at Esneh. Euergetes II. (Ptolemy IX.) built the little temple which stands on the western side of the temple of Khons at Karnak, and here and there engraved his cartouche on unoccupied corners at Medinet--Abou, at Deir-el-Bahari and at Karnak. Under him the temples of Philæ and of Edfou were enlarged, and that of Ombos and the speos were commenced.

Soter II. (Ptolemy X.) and Alexander (Ptolemy XI.) followed the steps of their predecessors and paid especial attention to Edfou. The latter prince founded Denderah. At Ombos, at Edfou, at Denderah and at Philæ, numerous traces are found of Dionysius (Ptolemy XIII.), while Cæsarion, the son of Cleopatra, figures at Denderah and at Erment.

When Egypt had become Roman, the emperors reigned there with the title of successors of the Pharaohs, and founded the XXXIVth and last dynasty. The emperors followed the traditions of the Ptolemies. Augustus, Tiberius, Caligula, Claudius and Nero continued the decorations of Denderah, and Tiberius founded its magnificent pronaos. The names of the same princes are found at Philæ and at Esneh. Nero's name also appears at Ombos. Nerva figures at Esneh, Trajan on the *Mammisi* of Denderah, Adrian at Philæ, and Marcus Aurelius at Esneh. Decius (A.D. 250) is the last emperor whose name is recorded on the monuments. He abruptly closes the list which is never to open again.

To sum up, those who do not wish to go any deeper into the subject may content themselves with remembering the names of the following dynasties and localities :—

IVth dynasty.—The Pyramids.
IVth and Vth dynasties.—Sakkârah.
XIIth dynasty.—Beni-Hassan. Necropolis of Abydos.
XIIIth dynasty.—Necropolis of Abydos.
XVIIIth, XIXth, and XXth dynasties.—Thebes on both banks of the Nile.
XXIInd dynasty.—The wall of the Bubastites at Karnak.

XXVth dynasty.—The small temple of Sabacon on the north side of Karnak.

XXVIth dynasty.—The columns at Karnak and at Luxor.

XXVIIth dynasty.—The Hamamât rocks.

XXXIInd dynasty.—The gateway at Elephantine. The granite sanctuary at Karnak.

XXXIIIrd dynasty.—The Ptolemies at Denderah, at Erment, at Esneh, at Ombos, and at Philæ.

XXXIVth dynasty.—The Roman Emperors at Denderah and at Esneh.

Of all those royal families, the IVth, the XII$_{th}$, the XVIIIth, the XIXth, and the Ptolemies have undoubtedly left the most numerous marks of their presence on the Egyptian soil.

F.—There is no need to enlarge upon the importance of the monuments that cover the banks of the Nile. They are the witnesses of Egypt's former greatness, and, so to speak, the patents of her ancient nobility. They represent in the eyes of strangers the tattered pages of the archives of one of the most glorious nations in the world.

But the higher the esteem in which we hold Egypt's monuments, the more it behoves us to preserve them with care. On their preservation partly depends the progress of those interesting studies which have for their object the history of ancient Egypt. Moreover, they are worthy of being preserved, not only for the sake of all such among us as appreciate them, but also for the sake of future Egyptologists. Five hundred years hence Egypt should still be able to show to the scholars who shall visit her the same monuments that we are now describing. The amount of information already obtained from the deciphering of hieroglyphs, though this science is still in its infancy, is already immense. What will it be when several generations of savants shall have studied those admirable ruins, of which one may truly say that the more they are known, the more they repay the labour bestowed upon them?

We therefore earnestly beg again and again all travellers in Upper Egypt to abstain from the childish practice of writing their names on the monuments. Let any one, for instance, visit Tih's tomb, at Sakkárah, and he will rest satisfied that this tomb has actually suffered more damage by the hand of tourists, during the last ten years, than it had during the whole of the previous six thousand years of its existence. Sethi I.'s beautiful tomb at Bab-el-Molouk is almost entirely disfigured, and it is all we can do to prevent the evil from increasing. M. Ampère, who visited Egypt in 1844, has, perhaps, overstepped the mark in the following lines extracted from his journal; yet we will transcribe them to show to what opprobrium those travellers expose themselves who thoughtlessly engrave their names on the monuments: "The first thing that strikes one on approaching the monument (Pompey's Pillar) is the number of names traced in gigantic characters by travellers, who have thus impertinently engraved a record of their obscurity on the time-honoured column. Nothing can be more silly than this mania, borrowed from the Greeks, which disfigures the monuments when it does not altogether destroy them. In many places, hours of patient toil have been expended in carving on the granite the large letters which dishonour it. How can any one give himself so much trouble to let the world know that an individual, perfectly unknown, has visited a monument, and that this unknown individual has mutilated it?" We recommend the perusal of the above lines to the young American traveller who, in 1870, visited all the ruins in Upper Egypt with a pot of *tar* in one hand and a brush in the other, leaving on all the temples the indelible and truly disgraceful record of his passage.*

G.—We have no advice to give to those travellers who wish to purchase antiquities and to take them home as souvenirs of their visit to Egypt. They will find more than one excellent factory at Luxor.

But to travellers who wish really to turn their journey to some account, we would recommend the search after papyri. In fact, there is nothing in the way of monuments more precious than a papyrus. One knows fairly well what may

* As to the two Dutch officials, the one an admiral, the other a consul-general, who have thought it right to apprise unborn generations of their visit to the temples in 1868, by writing their names and full titles in huge letters over the entrance gate of Denderah and in other conspicuous places, the translator must beg leave to say that men parading such titles ought to seek a more honourable way of transmitting their names to posterity.

be expected from a temple or from a tomb; but with the papyrus one is in the dark. In fact, such a papyrus might be discovered as would prove of more importance than an entire temple : and certain it is that if ever one of those discoveries that bring about a revolution in science should be made in Egyptology, the world will be indebted for it to a papyrus.

As all excavations are interdicted in Egypt and no permissive firman has ever been given, one might imagine that opportunities of purchasing papyri can never present themselves. Such, however, is not the case. All travellers in Upper Egypt must have seen fellahs working in those parts of the ruins where the crude-brick walls are crumbling into powder. What they are seeking is the dust which comes from the crumbling bricks, and which they use for manure. Now and then, however, a piece of good luck awaits them, and it is not an uncommon occurrence for a papyrus to be found in this manure. Nor must it be forgotten that, in spite of all prohibitions, clandestine searches are made, particularly at Thebes, and in this way also, among many other monuments, papyri may be discovered. It is for the traveller to make inquiries and to examine into the matter, not at Thebes only, but at all the stations where the *dahabeah* stops. The fine collection of Mr. Harris, at Alexandria, was formed in no other manner; and it was by mere accident that Madame d'Orbiney purchased the papyrus, now in the British Museum, which has rendered her name famous. In the present state of Egyptology, no greater service can be rendered to science than in securing any papyrus which accidentally falls into the hands of the fellahs, and which, sooner or later, must be entirely lost, if not thus preserved from destruction.

DESCRIPTION OF THE MONUMENTS.

THE railway which connects Cairo with Alexandria has reduced the latter city to a mere station on the route to Egypt from Marseilles, from Brindisi, from Trieste, or from Southampton. Travellers seldom stop now at Alexandria, and the real Egyptian journey commences at Cairo.

People visit Egypt because Egypt is the East, because Egypt is one of those illustrious countries which every man of refined culture feels it incumbent upon him to visit; but travellers would certainly be far less numerous if beyond Cairo there were not the still greater attraction of the glorious ruins of Upper Egypt.

Some travellers pass the first Cataract and proceed as far as Wády-Halfa. But the greater number stop at Assouán, and we also shall make the lovely island of Philæ the extreme limit of our journey on the Nile, in this Handbook.

The Upper Egypt railway at present extends to Siout, but that is practically of little avail; for at the end of the railway journey, even if the roadways were not to fail him, the traveller would find neither carriages, nor horses, nor any animals for riding, capable of sustaining a long and continuous journey. There remains then but one other mode of journeying, and that is along the Nile itself, which, in fact, is the one high road of Egypt. Therefore, immediately on his arrival at Cairo, the traveller would do well to take steps to secure either the dahabeah or the steamer which is to convey him throughout his journey.

But while the necessary preparations are going on, there is plenty to be seen in Cairo itself, and many an antiquity to be studied in the immediate vicinity, which will well repay a visit.

It is with these antiquities that we will begin our description.

EXCURSIONS
IN THE ENVIRONS OF CAIRO.

In the immediate vicinity of Cairo are found the ruins of two equally famous cities, Heliopolis and Memphis. The former is situated to the north-east of Cairo, on the right bank of the Nile, and the latter to the south-west, on the left bank.

The ruins of Heliopolis consist only of an immense inclosure, in the centre of which stands an obelisk. The ruins of Memphis comprise, besides the town properly so called, of which the remains are seen at Mitrahyneh, two vast cemeteries, namely the Pyramids and Sakkáarh.

Heliopolis, the Pyramids, Mitrahyneh, and Sakkárah, these then are the four localities of which we will give the description in this first chapter.

I.—HELIOPOLIS.

A carriage-road leads from Cairo to Heliopolis, passing by the palace of the Abbassieh, one of the residences of the Khedive, and by Matarieh, a village rendered famous by a miraculous well and a sycamore, known by the name of the *Virgin's tree.*

Matarieh is distant eight kilometres, or five English miles, from Cairo, and about half a mile further on are the ruins of Heliopolis.

Heliopolis was called *An* in Egyptian, or *On* in Hebrew. It was pre-eminently the city of *Ra*, or the city of the Sun; hence its Greek appellation. In ancient classical times Heliopolis enjoyed the reputation of being a sacerdotal city, celebrated for its college of priests. Solon, Plato, and Eudoxus studied there. Not that Heliopolis was either an extensive or a populous city, although a census taken under Rameses III. ascribes to one only of its temples a population of twelve thousand inhabitants.

The history of Heliopolis may be written in a few lines. The edifice " of barbarous construction," of which Strabo speaks, must have resembled in its architecture the temple of Armachis at the Pyramids of Geezeh, which proves that this city was already in existence under the Ancient Empire. Usertasen's obelisk, which is still standing, connects Heliopolis with the XIIth dynasty, and some blocks of stone, discovered during our excavations in 1858, further show that Thothmes III. enlarged one of its temples. When then did the decline of Heliopolis begin? Was it through the fury of Cambyses, as Strabo asserts, that its edifices were laid low? We cannot tell. Anyhow, Strabo, who visited Egypt only a few years before our era, describes it as almost a wilderness, and nothing now remains of it but the inclosing wall of the principal temple and the obelisk which stands in the centre. We speak advisedly when we say "the inclosing wall of the principal temple," for the high and extensive walls which form the enceinte of Heliopolis must not be mistaken for the walls of the city itself. It is true one may still see round the obelisk, and even at some distance from it, remains of demolished walls and vestiges of dwellings, which one is quite prepared to imagine are the remains of the houses of the city. But what occurred at Medinet-Abou, at Denderah, at Abydos and in many other places, took place also at Heliopolis. When their religion was abolished, the Egyptians, having become Christians, that is to say Copts, made use of the sacred edifices as habitations, and the precincts of the temples, until then considered as inviolable and holy, were covered with the dwellings of the people. The ruins, then, that surround the obelisk at Heliopolis are not the ruins of the ancient city, but those of the Coptic town which, at the downfall of the ancient gods of Egypt, replaced the pagan constructions,* and the large encircling wall, which marks their limit, extensive though it be,† is but the enceinte of the temple.

As for the obelisk itself, it should be regarded with interest, for it is the oldest in Egypt. It bears, in fact, the cartouches of Usertasen I., the second king of the XIIth dynasty. It is a little more than sixty-six English feet high. Formerly a casing of copper, of pyramidal form, covered its point, which still existed in the time of Abd-el-Latyf.‡

* Of the town, properly so called, nothing now remains. One may generally recognise the site of ancient cities by the grey or red heaps of rubbish formed by the crumbling of the brick-built houses one over the other, and these mounds are grouped in regular order round the vast encircling walls, in the centre of which stood the temples. But there is nothing of the sort here. Like Memphis, Heliopolis has paid the penalty of its proximity to Cairo, and the city has entirely disappeared.

† It measures about four thousand English feet by three thousand.

‡ An Arab doctor of Bagdad who visited Egypt about 1190 A.D.

A second obelisk completed with this one the decoration of the principal frontage of the temple, for which these two monoliths had been erected; but it was already fallen down and broken in two in the days of the Arabian historian we have just named,* and now it has entirely disappeared.

II.—THE PYRAMIDS.

The excursion to the Pyramids, like the excursion to Heliopolis, is usually made by carriage. The route lies through the new quarter of Cairo, called after its founder, *Ismaïlia*. The Nile is crossed by the Kasr-el-Nil bridge,

* This is the passage from Abd-el-Latyf: "It is in this city that are found the two famous obelisks called *Pharaoh's two needles*. These obelisks consist of a square base, six cubits long and six cubits wide, and of about the same height, resting firmly on its foundation. Above this base rises a square column of pyramidal form. . . . Its summit is covered with a sort of funnel-shaped casing of copper, which descends about three cubits from the top. This copper, from the effects of rain and the lapse of years, has rusted and turned green, and this green rust has discoloured the shaft of the obelisk. Its entire surface is covered with the sort of writing of which we have been speaking. I noticed that one of these obelisks had fallen down, and by the enormity of its own weight was broken in two; the copper which covered its summit had been removed."

and one soon enters the charming road constructed by his highness the Khedive, which leads from Geezeh to the foot of the Pyramids. From the Esbekyeh to the Pyramids the distance in a straight line is twelve kilometres, or about seven miles and a half. There are 8,300 metres, or 5 miles 280 yards from the banks of the Nile to the tableland on which stand the monuments we are about to describe.

The admiration in which the Pyramids have been held for so many centuries, and which has gained for them a place among the seven wonders of the world, is indeed well deserved. It must be confessed, however, that this admiration is not generally felt when the visitor first reaches the foot of these far-famed monuments. The fact is, the immensity of the surrounding desert and the want of some point of comparison effectually diminish the apparent size of the Pyramids, and prevent their being at first sight thoroughly appreciated. But they soon grow upon one, and assume their true proportions. And then one experiences a feeling of amazement at the immensity of those constructions. One sees in them the most lofty, the most durable, the most stupendous monuments under heaven that have ever been erected by the hand of man. The Pyramids are already six or seven thousand years old, but there is no reason why one hundred thousand years hence they should not be in the same state as we see them at the present day, provided no ignorant or profane hand be laid against them.

The three great Pyramids are the tombs of Cheops, of Chephren, and of Mycerinus; the smaller ones are the tombs of members of the families of those kings. The Great Pyramid was formerly 146 metres high (479 English feet), but in its present state it measures only 138 metres (about 453 English feet); its cube is of no less than 2,562,576 metres, and it covers an area of more than eleven English acres. All the stories which in accordance with Herodotus have been told about the hatred those kings had brought upon themselves, in consequence of the drudgery inflicted upon the Egyptians who worked in the construction of the Pyramids, may now be considered mere idle tales. The contemporaneous monuments—witnesses far more worthy of belief than Herodotus—tell us, in fact, that during their lifetime and after their death, Cheops and Chephren, equally with all other kings, were honoured with a special worship. As for Mycerinus, he was so pious a king that he is quoted in the *Ritual* as the author of one of the most renowned works in the religious literature of Egypt.

As to the especial purpose for which the Pyramids were intended, it is doing violence to all that we know of Egypt, to all that archæology has taught us on the subject of the monumental habits of this country, to imagine for a moment that they could ever have been intended for aught else but tombs. The Pyramids are tombs, massive, entire, everywhere hermetically sealed, even in their most carefully constructed passages; without windows, without doors, without external openings of any kind. They are the gigantic and ever impenetrable sepulchre of a mummy, and even had one of them exhibited in its interior an accessible passage from whence, as from the bottom of a well, astronomical observations could have been made, that Pyramid would not have been in 'accordance with its purpose. In vain shall it be said that the four sides turned to the different points of the compass denote an astronomical intention; the four sides are thus set because they are dedicated for mythological reasons to the four cardinal points, and in a monument so carefully constructed as a Pyramid, a side dedicated to the north, for example, could not by any possibility be turned to any other point but the north. The Pyramids, then, are nothing but tombs, and their enormous bulk could not be held as an argument against this theory, since there are some which are scarcely eighteen feet high. Moreover, there does not exist in Egypt a single pyramid that is not the centre of a necropolis, a fact which confirms in the most emphatic manner the character of these monunents.

What remains now of the Pyramids is only the nucleus. Originally they were covered with a smooth casing which has entirely disappeared, and they terminated in a sharp point. Being tombs hermetically sealed, each one of the Pyramids, or at least each of those that served as the sepulchre of a king, possessed an exterior temple which was built within a few yards of the eastern façade. The king, deified as a sort of incarnation of the divinity, was here worshipped. The three great Pyramids of Geezeh possess, like all other Pyramids, an exterior temple.

What proves that Pyramids were monuments hermetically sealed is that, when Amrou wanted to penetrate into the Great Pyramid, he was only able to succeed by perforating the northern side by force, very nearly in the axis, which caused him accidentally to come upon the ascending passage of the interior. As at that time the outer covering was still perfect and consequently there was no accumulation of rubbish at its base, it may safely be inferred that the entrance itself was not visible from the outside.

About six hundred yards to the S.E. of the Great Pyramid is the Sphinx. The Sphinx is a natural rock, to which has been given, more or less accurately, the external appearance of that mystic animal. The head alone has been sculptured. The body is formed of the rock itself, supplemented, where defective, by a somewhat clumsy masonry of limestone. The total height of the monument is 19 metres 80 centimetres, equal to 65 English feet. The ear measures 6 feet 5 inches; the nose 5 feet 10 inches; and the mouth 7 feet 8 inches. The face, in its widest part, across the cheek, is 4 metres 15 centimetres, that is, 13 feet 7 inches.

Its origin is still a matter of doubt. At one time it was supposed to be a monument of the the reign of Thothmes IV. (XVIIIth dynasty). But we know now, thanks to a stone in the Boolák Museum, that the Sphinx was already in existence when Cheops (who preceded Chephren) gave orders for the repairs which this stone commemorates. It must also be remembered that the Sphinx is the colossal image of an Egyptian god called *Armachis*.

Near the Sphinx is a singular construction which, even to a greater degree than the Sphinx itself, is an enigma to Egyptologists. It is certain that this construction is as ancient as the Pyramids. But is it a temple, or is it a tomb? Its external appearance, it must be confessed, is rather that of a tomb. From a distance it must have presented the appearance of a *mastaba*, scarcely exceeding in size those which are actually found, for example, at Abousir and Sakkárah. In one of the chambers of the interior there are six compartments, placed one above the other, which certainly seem to have been constructed, like those of the third Pyramid and of the Mastabat-el-Faraoun, for the reception of mummies. Moreover, the place does not differ essentially from that of certain other tombs which are found in the vicinity. It may therefore be fairly argued that the monument in question was a tomb, without violating any rules of criticism; can the contrary opinion, which calls it a temple, be equally well supported? It is true, the Ancient Empire having left us no other temple with which to compare this one, it is not unnatural to suppose that at this remote period Egyptian temples might have been constructed on the extraordinary plan of the one we are now considering. Nor is it unnatural either to assume that, since the Sphinx is a god, the adjoining monument may be the temple of that god. But are these arguments sufficient? And, after all, to put the case plainly, is the monument an annex of the Sphinx, or is not rather the Sphinx an annex of the monument? Does not the whole of this represent a very ancient tomb, adorned, for the sake of greater dignity, with a colossal statue of a god? The question is pending.

We need hardly remind the reader that the spot we are now visiting is one of the cemeteries of Memphis, just as Père Lachaise is one of the cemeteries of Paris. The tombs therein date from almost every period; those of the Ancient Empire, however, predominate. The latter most frequently take the form of the *mastaba*, a sort of truncated pyramid built of enormous stones and covering, as with a massive lid, the well at the bottom of which reposed the mummy. The visitor may observe two or three good specimens near the eastern side of the Great Pyramid; but a better opportunity of studying this sort of monument will be afforded us at Saḳḳárah.

To this description of the Pyramids we here add a plan which will serve as a guide to the traveller who, being anxious to escape from the deafening cries of the guides and their tiresome demands for *baksheesh*, may feel induced to make a somewhat serious study of the interior of the most important of these monuments. As we have already stated, the outer casing formerly concealed the entrance to the Pyramid, and it is evident that in the original design this entrance was to remain for ever closed. At the present time the Pyramid is entered by a square hole on the thirteenth layer of stone, at about sixty feet from the ground.

This description being intended for the traveller who visits the interior of the Pyramid with the plan in his hand, it is not necessary to give many details. A is a subterranean chamber, at present inaccessible. B is called the Queen's Chamber, a title justified by no tradition whatever. C is called the King's Chamber. D is a sort of landing intersected by two grooves, into which glided, once upon a time, that is to say when the royal mummy had just been deposited in the sarcophagus, the two massive blocks which were to close to all eternity the entrance of the chamber. E, F, G and H are the communicating passages. I is a landing-place into which leads the forced passage of the Caliph Amrou. J is the mysterious well which has so long put the sagacity of discoverers to so severe a test. Such is the interior of the Pyramid.

But now, what was the purpose of all these apparently inextricable passages and rooms? Evidently everything was done to deceive the future violators of the Pyramid, and to throw them off the scent as to the actual position of the mummy. For let us suppose that the entrance hidden under the outer casing has been discovered. A first obstacle will present itself, namely, the blocks with which corridor H is fitted up. If these blocks be broken and a passage

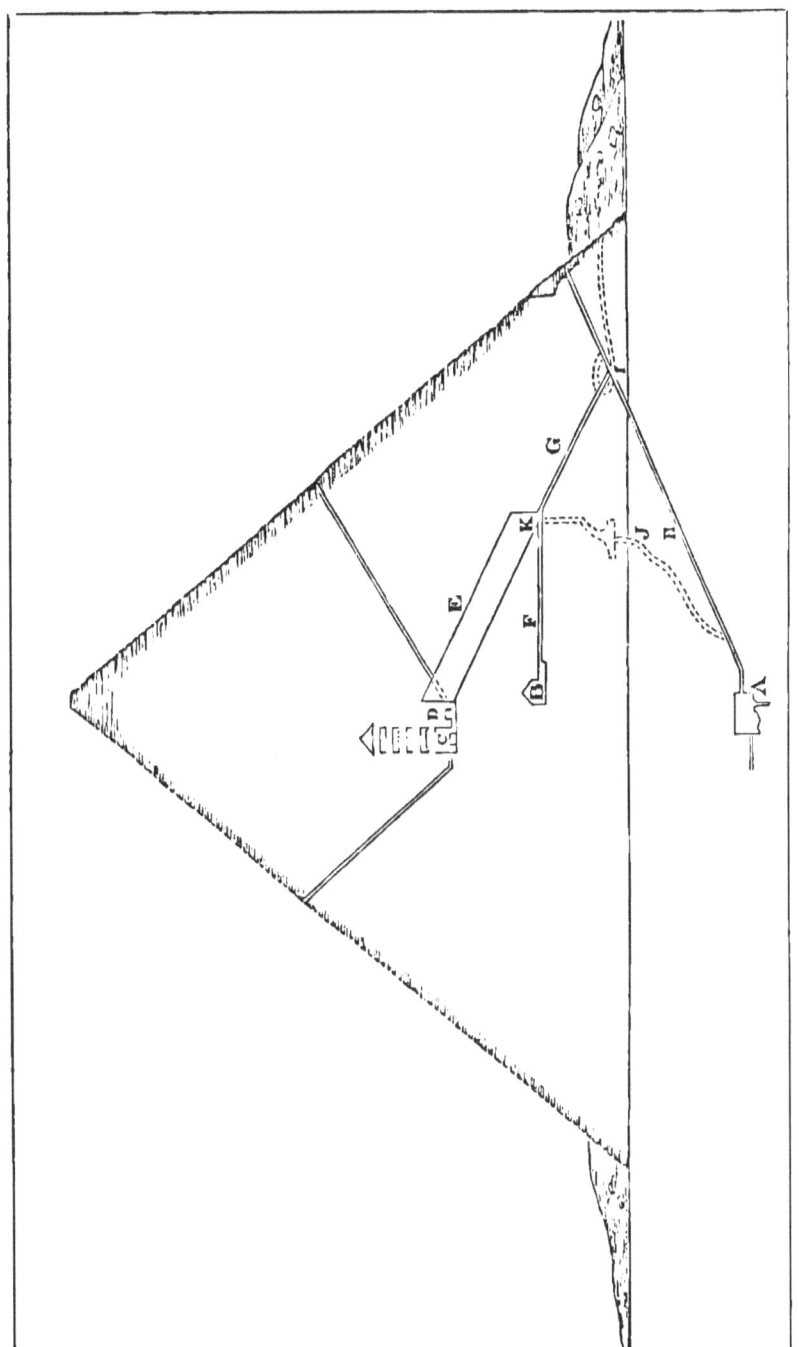

THE GREAT PYRAMID.

successfully forced, chamber A will be reached. If it is now discovered that chamber A is not the true chamber of the Pyramid, corridor H must next be sounded at all points to discover the unknown spot from whence the passage, supposed to be the correct one, branches off. But this time one has to do with blocks of granite, since two of these blocks are still in their place (landing-place I). This obstacle, which is not to be broken, must then be turned, and one comes upon the ascending corridor G at the end of which the landing-place K would not have been disposed as we find it at the present day. It would be completely blocked, as also would be the aperture of the well. If the passage is forced, it is quite natural to follow the flagstones, and the explorer will find himself in corridor F without suspecting that a second ascending corridor runs over his head. Chamber B is thus reached. Here fresh doubts will arise as to the real character of this chamber, and fresh efforts will be made to ascertain where the next bifurcation takes place. The point of connection is hit upon after a while, and the *corbellated* corridor E is gone through, when at length the true chamber is reached, the two grooves presenting no serious obstacle. There is nothing, even to the well, which is not explained in this manner of accounting for the internal distribution of the monument. During the construction of the Pyramid, blocks of granite of the same dimensions as corridor G were deposited in the corbellated corridor E. The Pyramid being finished, and the mummy laid in its place, these blocks would be allowed to slide by their own weight down corridor G ; the landing-place K would then be blocked up, and the workmen would descend by the well and return to the open air by the corridor H, which in its turn would be obstructed by blocks introduced through the external entrance of the monument. Let us add that experience in excavations authorises this explanation to a certain extent. Indeed, it is no uncommon thing to find tombs where a false scent has intentionally diverted the attention of the would-be violators of the pit in which the mummy is reposing.*

III.—MITRAHENNY.

Mitrahenny lies on the road from Cairo to Sakkárah. Both villages therefore are visited in

* Examine with this view the two great Pyramids of Dashoor. Here again every endeavour has been made to deceive those who might seek to rifle the monument.

the same excursion; the first is passed just before reaching the second.

The traveller who wishes to visit Mitrahenny and Sakkárah can wait until his dahabeah is ready, and then make Bedreshayn his first halting-place on his journey up the Nile.

If, however, he should prefer making the excursion from Cairo, there are two routes from which he can choose. He can either hire donkeys at Cairo and ride the whole way to the colossus of Mitrahenny (the donkey boys know the way and would serve as guides), or he can send forward the donkeys to Bedreshayn which is the nearest station to Mitrahenny on the Upper Egypt railway, in which case he would take a carriage from Cairo to Geezeh, and would continue his journey by train from Geezeh. This is the favourite route, especially with those who have not much time to spare or who dread the fatigue of a long journey, to and fro, on donkeyback.

Memphis was in all probability the largest city in Egypt, and if, as we believe, the step-shaped Pyramid at Sakkárah belongs to the Ist dynasty, Memphis may assuredly boast of an antiquity that Thinis alone can rival. A palace " of barbarous construction " was to be found here as well as at Heliopolis.

Explorations have not confirmed the assertion of Strabo, who describes Memphis as reaching to the foot of the Libyan chain. Memphis, on the contrary, seems to have been shut in between the Bahr-Jousef on the one side and the Nile on the other, and thus to have been a city of an extremely elongated form, stretching to the north nearly as far as Geezeh and to the south to Schinbab, an extent which accounts for its cemeteries being scattered widely apart. Throughout the whole length of the space contained within the above boundaries are mounds, more or less arid, strewn here and there with blocks of granite and foundations of walls which emerge from the surface of the soil. On the most considerable of these mounds is situated the village of Mitrahenny, where once stood the famous temple of Phtah, the Vulcan of Greek tradition.

The history of Memphis is, on the whole, very much the same as that of Heliopolis. We have here, however, materials that Heliopolis could not yield. The still extant burial-grounds of Memphis (the Pyramids, Abousir, Sakḳárah and Dashoor) furnish us with abundant information on the history of that city during the different periods of its existence. Founded under the most ancient kings, the successors of Menes—flourishing under the IVth dynasty, that grand epoch which witnessed the rise of the Pyramids; equally prosperous under the Vth and the beginning of the VIth; neglected and abandoned under the XIth, XIIth and XIIIth dynasties, Memphis revived, like Egypt herself, as soon as the kings of the XVIIIth dynasty had succeeded in purging the national soil of its invaders. Taken and retaken by turns under the subsequent dynasties by the Assyrians, the Ethiopians and the Persians, Memphis recovered under the Greeks a portion of her ancient splendour, even though Strabo describes her at the time of his visit as being already deserted. The time, however, was approaching when nothing would be left of Memphis but ruins, and when the gloomy threatenings of Jeremiah should be literally fulfilled: "O daughter of Egypt, prepare thyself for captivity; for Memphis shall be laid waste; she shall be abandoned and shall become uninhabitable." And now nothing remains of the once proud city which through so many centuries exercised so profound an influence over the destinies of mankind—nothing but interminable mounds where only the date-palm can grow, besides here and there the *débris* of a wall, the shaft of a broken column, and mutilated statues half-hidden in the ground or buried in the mud.

Yet it must not be imagined that Memphis disappeared all at once, and as it were at one stroke, at the very same moment when the ancient Egyptian civilisation received its death-blow. It is even curious to see in Abd-el-Latyf in what state were the ruins of Memphis eight hundred years ago: "Let us pass now," says the Arab traveller, "to other vestiges of Egypt's greatness; I mean to the ruins of the ancient capital of that country. This capital was Memphis, the residence of the Pharaohs and the seat of government of the Kings of Egypt. Notwithstanding the enormous size of this city, and her exceeding great antiquity, in spite of the many vicissitudes of the various Governments to whose yoke she had successively submitted; notwithstanding the efforts made by various people to annihilate her by destroying the smallest vestige and defacing the slightest trace of her, carrying away the stones and materials of which she was built, laying waste her edifices, and mutilating the figures with which they were adorned; in spite also of what the lapse of four thousand years and even more must have added to so many other causes of destruction, her ruins still offer to the eye of the spectator an assemblage of wonders which astonish the mind, and which the most gifted writer would find it impossible to describe. The more one contemplates this city, the more does the admiration she inspires increase, and each successive visit to her ruins becomes a fresh cause of wonder and delight." A little further on, Abd-el-Latyf adds: " One sees on the same spot pedestals resting on enormous foundations. The quantity of stones proceeding from the demolition of the buildings seems to fill up the surface of these ruins; in some places bits of broken walls are still standing, . . . elsewhere nothing is to be seen but the foundations, or heaps of ruined fragments. I saw the arch of a very high door, the two side walls of which are formed each of a single stone, and the vault above, also formed of a single stone, had fallen down in front of the door. . . . As for the figures of idols which are found among those ruins, whether as regards their number or their enormous magnitude, it is something that baffles description, and of which one can hardly convey any idea; but what is still more worthy of admiration is the precision of their forms, the accuracy of their proportions and their great resemblance to nature. We found one which without its pedestal was more than thirty cubits high. . . . This statue was in a single block of red granite, covered with a red polish to which its antiquity seemed only to lend an additional freshness."

And still further on he says: "I saw two lions facing each other within a short distance; their aspect inspired awe; for notwithstanding their colossal size, infinitely larger than that of life, the sculptor had succeeded in preserving the truthfulness of form and of proportion. They have been broken and covered with earth."

It is impossible to peruse these lines, written by one of the most sagacious and the most truthful of Arabian historians, without bitterly regretting the treasures we have lost. Even Karnak, stripped as it has been for the last fifty years of all its riches, can give but a faint idea of what Memphis must have been at the end of the XIIth century, before the stones of its temples had one by one been swallowed up in the constructions of Cairo. But alas! there now remains nothing to be seen of Memphis, beyond the few following monuments:—

1. The hollow space, on the borders of which the traveller must pass as he reaches the ruins, and beyond which he perceives through a vista of trees the pointed summits of the Pyramids, is the lake of the temple of Vulcan. Close by is a colossus in pink granite, discovered in 1852 by Hekekyan-Bey. It represents Rameses II., and the superscribed cartouches are those of the immediate successors of that prince.

2. A few yards further on, to the south of the colossus, is a large stela, in white limestone, lying face upwards. It dates from the time of Apries (XXVIth dynasty). Apries had increased the endowment of the temple of Vulcan, and had enlarged the temple itself, for the service of which he had made several lakes or canals. The stela was intended to preserve the remembrance of those benefits.

3. Near to the isolated house in which have been stored away some broken statues discovered during our excavations is another colossus. This is in silicious limestone, and represents Rameses II. The statues of Rameses are so common that science would attach no importance to this one, were it not that the head, modelled with a gran-

deur of style which one never tires of admiring, is an authentic portrait of the celebrated conqueror of the XIXth dynasty.*

IV.—SAKKARAH.

Sakkárah is a village which gives its name to the necropolis near which it is situated. This necropolis is the most important, the most ancient, and yet at the same time the most modern of all the cemeteries of Memphis. It extends along the verge of the sands of the desert for about four miles and a half in length, with a breadth varying from a third of a mile to nearly one mile.

There is certainly not, at the present time, a single spot in the whole of the necropolis of Sakkárah that has not already been, over and

* This statue was discovered by Caviglia, about 1820, and was given by Mehemet Ali to the English Government. For nine months in every year it is under water. There is every reason to suppose that it stood facing the north, against a pylon of the temple of Vulcan of which not a vestige remains. A second colossus must have corresponded with this one on the other side of the entrance. For this second colossus, however, we have sought in vain. Examples of such an arrangement are found at Luxor and at Karnak, and the two colossi of the pylon at Luxor also represent Rameses.

over again, explored by excavations more or less ancient. It offers, in fact, a spectacle of utter devastation. Pits without number lie yawning at the feet of the passer-by. Dismantled brick walls, heaps of sand mingled with stones and particles of granite, encumber the traveller's path almost at every step. Here and there fragments of mummy-cloth borne along by the wind, or human bones drying and bleaching in the sun, warn us that we are in the region of the dead.

No less remarkable are the many pyramids with which the necropolis is covered. In the centre, forming as it were the nucleus of this vast *ensemble*, rises a pyramid curiously built in six gradients. If tradition may be trusted, and if the spot of which this pyramid is the centre is called *Ko-Komeh*, and if King Ouenephes really built his pyramid in a place called Ko-Komeh, then this step-shaped pyramid dates from the I[st] dynasty, and is consequently the most ancient known monument, not in Egypt only, but in the whole world. The other pyramids bear no date, and it is probable that the greater number of them have never been opened.*

* The step-shaped pyramid has been opened, but a recent falling in of part of the masonry has obstructed

The necropolis of Sakkârah is so vast that it is impossible to visit the whole of it. The monuments most frequently inspected are the *Serapeum*, the *Tomb of Tih*, and the *Tomb of Phtah-Hotep*.

A.—THE SERAPEUM.—The Serapeum is one of the edifices of Memphis rendered famous by a frequently quoted passage of Strabo, and by the constant mention made of it on the Greek papyri. It had long been sought for, and we had the good fortune to discover it in 1851.[*]

the entrance. To the S. of the necropolis is the *Mastabat--el-Faraoun*, a vast construction of royal origin, of which we discovered the entrance in 1859. Some quarry marks traced in red on the blocks employed in the masonry-work have left signs which seem to us to form the name of Ounas, one of the last kings of the Vth dynasty.

[*] Strabo, in his description of Memphis, expresses himself thus: "One finds also (at Memphis) a temple of Serapis in a spot so sandy that the wind causes the sand to accumulate in heaps, under which we could see many sphinxes, some of them almost entirely buried, others only partially covered; from which we may conjecture that the route leading to this temple might be attended with danger if one were surprised by a sudden gust of wind."

If Strabo had not written this passage, in all probability the Serapeum would to this day lie buried under the sands of the necropolis of Sakkârah. In 1850 I had

Apis, the living image of Osiris revisiting the earth, was a bull who, while he lived, had his temple at Memphis (Mitrahenny), and, when dead, had his tomb at Sakkárah. The palace which the bull inhabited in his lifetime was called the *Apieum;* the *Serapeum* was the name given to his tomb.

As far as we can judge by the remains found during our researches, the Serapeum resembled in appearance the other Egyptian temples, even those which were not funereal in their character. An avenue of sphinxes led up to it, and two

been commissioned by the French Government to visit the Coptic convents of Egypt, and to make an inventory of such manuscripts in Oriental languages as I should find there. I noticed at Alexandria, in M. Zizinia's garden, several sphinxes. Presently I saw more of these same sphinxes at Cairo, in Clot-Bey's garden. M. Fernandez had also a certain number of such sphinxes at Geezeh. Evidently there must be somewhere an avenue of sphinxes which was being pillaged. One day, attracted to Sakkárah by my Egyptological studies, I perceived the head of one of these same sphinxes obtruding itself from the sand. This one had never been touched, and was certainly in its original position. Close by lay a libation-table, on which was engraved in hieroglyphs an inscription to Osiris-Apis. The passage in Strabo suddenly occurred to my mind. The avenue which lay at my feet must be the one which led up to that Serapeum so long and so vainly sought for. But I had been sent to Egypt to make pylons stood before it, and it was surrounded by the usual inclosure. But what distinguished it from all other temples was that out of one of its chambers opened an inclined passage leading directly into the rock on which the temple was built, and giving access to vast subterranean vaults which were the *Tomb of Apis*.

The Serapeum, properly so called, no longer exists, and where it stood there is now nothing to be seen but a vast plain of sand mingled with fragments of stones scattered about in indescribable confusion. But the most beautiful and interesting part of the subterranean vault can still be visited.

The Tomb of Apis consists of three distinct
an inventory of manuscripts, not to seek for temples. My mind, however, was soon made up. Regardless of all risks, without saying a word, and almost furtively, I gathered together a few workmen, and the excavation began. The first attempts were hard indeed, but, before very long, lions and peacocks and the Grecian statues of the dromos, together with the monumental tablets or *stelæ* of the temple of Nectanebo, were drawn out of the sand, and I was able to announce my success to the French Government, informing them, at the same time, that the funds placed at my disposal for the researches after the manuscripts were entirely exhausted, and that a further grant was indispensable. Thus was begun the discovery of the Serapeum.

The work lasted four years. The Serapeum is a temple

parts which have no direct communication with one another.

The first and most ancient part carries us back as far as the XVIIIth dynasty and Amenophis III. It served as the burial-place of the sacred bulls up to the end of the XXth dynasty. Here the tombs are separate. Every dead Apis had his own sepulchral chamber hewn here and there, as it were at random, out of the rock. These chambers are now hidden under the sand, and were never possessed of any very great interest.

The second part comprises the tombs of Apis from the time of Sheshonk I. (XXIInd dynasty) to that of Tahraka (the last king of the XXVth dynasty). In this part a new system was adopted. Instead of isolated tombs, a long subterranean gallery was made, on each side of which mortu-

built without any regular plan, where all was conjecture, and where the ground had to be examined closely, inch by inch. In certain places the sand is, so to speak, fluid, and presents as much difficulty in excavating as if it were water which ever seeks its own level. Besides all this, difficulties arose between the French and the Egyptian Governments, which obliged me several times to discharge all my workmen. It was owing to these circumstances (to say nothing of other trials) that the work proved so long, and that I was compelled to spend four years in the desert—four years, however, I can never regret.

ary chambers were excavated, to be used whenever an Apis expired at Memphis. This gallery is also inaccessible now, the roof having in some places fallen in, and the remainder not being sufficiently secure to allow of its being visited by travellers.*

The third part is that which is now so well known. Its history begins with Psammetichus I. (XXVIth dynasty), and ends with the later Ptolemies. The same system of a common vault has been followed here as in the second part, only on a much grander scale. These galleries cover an extent of about 350 metres, or 1,150 English feet; and from one end to the other the great gallery measures 195 metres, or about 640 English feet. Moreover, granite sarcophagi have

* In approaching the entrance to the tomb of Apis by the ordinary path, one sees to the right, *i.e.* towards the N., a somewhat large circular hole. Here are to be found the vaults which preceded those we are about to visit. This hole was caused by the falling in of a portion of the stone-work. In blowing up the *débris* with gunpowder, we discovered, not an Apis, but a human mummy. A gold mask covered its face, and jewels of every description were arranged on its breast. All the inscriptions were in the name of Rameses' favourite son, who was for a long time governor of Memphis. It may therefore be reasonably supposed that it was here this prince was buried.

been used here. Their number throughout the whole extent of the galleries is 24. Of these only three bear any inscription, and they contain the names of Amasis (XXVIth dynasty), Cambyses and Khebasch (XXVIIth dynasty). A fourth, with cartouches without any name, most probably belongs to one of the last Ptolemies. As to their dimensions, they measure on an average 7 feet 8 inches in breadth, by 13 feet in length, and 11 feet in height; so that, allowing for the vacuum, these monoliths must weigh, one with the other, not less than 65 tons each.

Such are the three parts of the Tomb of Apis.

It is well known that the exploration of this tomb has furnished science with unhoped-for results. For what the traveller now sees of it is merely its skeleton. But the fact is that, although it had been rifled by the early Christians, the tomb, when first discovered, still possessed nearly all that it had ever contained that was not gold or other precious matter. There existed a custom which had especially contributed to enrich the tomb with valuable documents. On certain days in the year, or on the occasion of the death and funeral rites of an Apis, the inhabitants of Memphis came to pay a visit to the god in his burial-place. In memory of this act of piety they left a *stela*, *i.e.* a square-shaped stone, rounded at the top, which was let into one of the walls of the tomb, having been previously inscribed with an homage to the god in the name of his visitor and his family. Now these documents, to the number of about five hundred, were found, for the most part, in their original position (see especially the entrance chamber to the N.); and as many of them were dated according to the fashion of the time, that is with the year, month and day of the reigning king, a comparison of these inscribed tablets must necessarily prove of the greatest importance, especially in fixing chronology.

B.—TOMBS OF TIH AND OF PHTAH-HOTEP.— After visiting the Serapeum, the traveller usually turns his steps towards one or more of those tombs of the Ancient Empire in which the necropolis of Sakkárah is so rich. We will select for description those of Tih and of Phtah-Hotep.

Generally speaking, a tomb of the Ancient Empire may be recognised externally by a small building having the form of a *mastabah*.* This *mastabah* consists of three parts, viz. : 1st, one or more chambers, sometimes with the addition of a *serdab*, a sort of narrow passage concealed in the thickness of the masonry—these chambers being accessible at all times through a doorway opening upon one of the streets of the necropolis ; 2nd, a vertical pit opening out of one of the chambers; 3rd, a sepulchral chamber hollowed out in the rock, wherein the mummy reposes.

The *serdab* never bears any inscriptions ; the chambers, on the contrary, are almost always decorated, and these representations are too interesting not to arrest our attention.

Strangely enough, everything here is as little funereal as possible. In the tombs of other periods, as we shall see in more than one instance at Bab-el-Molouk, an army of strange fantastic gods has invaded the walls of the chamber. The defunct is there seen actually in the other world, and in a world peopled with

* The reader already knows that under the Ancient Empire the tombs of private individuals were generally in the form of the *mastabah*, by which we mean a sort of pyramid, truncated near the base, and which from a distance presents the appearance of an enormous sarcophagus lid.

beings mostly impossible to describe. But here we have nothing of the kind, and we would look in vain for a single representation of the divinity on the walls. The defunct is in this world and not in the other.* He is represented standing, or sometimes seated, with the staff of office in his hand. His wife is by his side, and his children close by; his servants are standing before him, and it altogether looks as if he were still of this world.

Let us try and fathom the meaning of these pictures, and we shall find the principle we have alluded to more and more forcibly brought out. On the lintel of the entrance to each tomb, whenever this part is not altogether destroyed, which is unfortunately too often the case, is a somewhat long inscription which serves as a sort of introduction to the monument. The name and titles of the defunct are set forth, and

* See the reservations brought to bear upon these ideas in the *Introduction*, page 9. The present description of the tombs of Sakkârah dates from 1869, whilst the *Introduction* was written in 1872. This divergence of opinion shows through what stages science must needs pass: and it may be that on further inquiry into the facts thus far ascertained, or through the discovery of fresh data, we shall be compelled once more to modify our view on this subject.

then follows an invocation which sums up, so to speak, the pictures that are to be found in such numbers in the interior. In this invocation Anubis, the guardian of tombs, is entreated, 1st, to grant to the personage named a worthy sepulture in the necropolis, after a long and happy life; 2nd, to befriend the defunct during his journey through the regions beyond the grave; 3rd, to secure to him through all eternity the proper paying of what the text calls "the funereal gifts." Now, it is especially to these three subjects of invocation that the pictures in the interior refer; for every one of them may be included under either of the three following heads:—

1. *Scenes relating to the personage while still living.*—The tomb of Tih offers several of these pictures, most interesting to study. The defunct is in his home. In the narrow entrance passage on the southern wall some women of his household are dancing before him; musicians are playing on various instruments, and singers accompany them, beating time with their hands. On the northern wall of the large chamber the defunct is shooting in the marshes; he is standing upright on a bark made of papyrus reeds; with one hand he holds some call-birds and with

the other he lets fly, over the aquatic birds dispersed among the tall reeds, a curved stick which whirls round and round. Crouching in the water on which the bark is sailing are hippopotami and crocodiles. Some of his servants are trying to catch them. One curious episode is a combat between two of these amphibious animals; the crocodile is vanquished. Close by, a servant of the household is hooking a hippopotamus with a sort of harpoon—a scene which forcibly recalls to one's mind those two verses of Job (chap. xli. 1, 2), " Canst thou draw out leviathan with an hook? or his tongue with a cord which thou lettest down? Canst thou put an hook into his nose? or bore his jaw through with a thorn?" The figure on the tomb deserves special attention. Another scene represents the shooting of certain aquatic birds by the servitors of the defunct. Further on, upon the same northern wall, are charming representations of country life. Cows are passing over a ford; calves are feeding in a meadow; herdsmen are conducting a flock of goats. Equally curious are the agricultural pictures on the eastern wall of the same chamber. The corn is reaped; it is gathered into stacks; it is threshed and tied into sheaves, with which asses are laden. At each of these varied scenes the defunct is present, either seated or standing, in the attitude of command. Here (on the eastern wall) he witnesses the building of his barks; there (on the southern wall) he superintends carpenters making furniture for his house; elsewhere (on the western side of the small entrance passage) large ships with distended sails, and barks manned by rowers, float on the Nile, bent on his errands. In fact, everything in these pictures shows the realisation of the first petition in favour of the defunct over the entrance to the tomb. Tih evidently leads a happy and prosperous life on earth, the very ideal that must have been conceived by a people entirely devoted to agricultural pursuits. He is surrounded by his family and his servants, and he attains, as the inscription records, "a happy and prolonged old age." (Compare the inscriptions of the tomb of Phtah-Hotep).

2. *Scenes relating to the death of the personage.*—This is the least communicative of the three parts. The defunct, standing erect in a bark, watches the conveyance of his own mummy into the necropolis. But this representation does not occur frequently, and one easily understands the

sort of euphemism which compels the constructor of the tomb to pass lightly over this part of the decoration. Moreover, it is worthy of remark that the conveyance of the mummy is the only really funereal scene which these pictures offer us. We see the defunct conducted to his burial-place, but we do not follow him to the regions beyond the grave. All the representations of the tomb refer to the present world; not one ventures to penetrate beyond that mysterious portal which separates our frail perishable life from the life eternal.

3. *Scenes relating to the bringing in of funereal gifts.*—The chambers we are now visiting were open to all comers, and on certain fête-days the relatives of the deceased met together here. Now, a universal custom made it incumbent upon those relatives to bring to the tomb offerings of all sorts—bread, wine, the produce of the fields, and the limbs of animals slaughtered outside. These are what our inscription calls " the funereal gifts." The pictures relating to the bringing in of these gifts are numerous. Both walls of the little chamber on the right of the entrance passage of Tih's tomb are covered with scenes of this nature: servants carrying on their heads or shoulders, or on their extended hands,

victuals, flowers, and trays laden with vases. On the eastern wall of the same entrance passage has been represented the slaughtering of the bullocks intended to constitute an important part of the funereal gifts. In the interior of the tomb, on the lowest register of the northern wall, is a long file of women driving various animals and carrying couffes or frail baskets on their heads. The various farms of the defunct are thus symbolised, and are all made to contribute to the accomplishment of the ceremony for bringing in those offerings which are intended to figure in kind within the innermost chamber of the tomb.

Scenes of this description are most vividly conveyed in the tomb of Phtah-Hotep. There (on the western wall, between the two stelæ) the defunct is seated, and before him passes a regular procession of servants, bringing offerings. At their head march priests chanting sacred hymns, while behind them other servants of the household heap up on a table the offerings destined to the ceremony. Phtah-Hotep himself receives the gifts, and carries to his lips a vase containing one of the substances which figure in "the bringing in of the funereal gifts."

We should be carried away too far if we attempted to describe the many pictures, so varied in their composition, which adorn the walls of the tombs of Tih and Phtah-Hotep. What we wish to impress on the visitor's mind is the general meaning of these pictures, that he may thereby realise the character of that part of the tomb in which they are placed. Let us remember that we are in the interior of a *mastabah*, on a level, however, with the surrounding plain. There is nothing mournful here, nothing to remind us of death. The deceased seems to be in his home; he receives his relatives and the people of his household. Moreover, he himself commenced the tomb in his lifetime, and had those scenes sculptured on the walls which we have just endeavoured to interpret.

"The Egyptians," says Diodorus, "call their habitations hostelries, because of the short space of time during which they sojourn there; whilst they speak of their tombs as eternal abodes." Such, indeed, is the true character of the monuments we are examining. The house, the farm, the cattle, the fields, the harvest, everything is here represented, and by the solidity of its construction the tomb becomes truly an "eternal abode."

As to the soul, as to that life beyond the grave which the Egyptians have made the basis of their faith, and which is here altogether wanting, another part of the tomb is assigned to it. But no one may enter therein, and it must remain for ever hidden. This is the sepulchral chamber, for ever lost to view under the ground, at the bottom of a pit, the entrance of which is carefully concealed from all eyes. There lies the mummy, but there also is the *Ritual*. The defunct has crossed the awful threshold, and is now in that mysterious world where gods and pure spirits dwell.

To sum up, a Sakkârah tomb consists of an external building which incloses three distinct parts, viz.: 1st, some chambers accessible at all times and most frequently decorated with sculptures; 2nd, a vertical pit * hidden from all eyes,

* It so happens that the tomb of Tih offers a very rare exception to this rule. The pit, as may now be seen in the centre of the court, is not vertical, but slopes down like the passage of a pyramid. The principle, however, is the same. This inclined passage was filled to the very bottom with blocks of stone. The sarcophagus is in limestone, and bears no inscription whatever.

into which no one at the present time can descend without ropes; 3rd, a subterranean vault where lies the mummy. Let us add that all the other tombs one meets with in Egypt are constructed on the same principle.

JOURNEY

INTO UPPER EGYPT.

A FEW years ago, the only means of visiting Upper Egypt was by *dahabiah*. But now steamers start on certain days and accommodate a goodly number of passengers.

Thoroughly to enjoy the journey, however, it should be made in a dahabiah. For there you feel at home, and, open to any impression that may arise, you can stop where you please; you can land and shoot, or visit the villages, and never leave the temples and monuments, until you feel you have done justice to them.

It is true you are sometimes too much at the mercy of the wind, but no one should undertake the journey in a dahabiah who has not plenty of time to spare. To the traveller, then, who wishes really to see and to know Egypt we recommend the dahabiah. As to the steamer, we have little advice to give. Everything on board is clean and comfortable; meals are served at regular hours; and at regular hours also the temples and monuments are visited and admired in company with a dragoman and a number of fellow-travellers whom one has never seen before. Egypt, however, cannot be seen and known in this manner; only a vague idea of her many beauties and her vast interest can thus be obtained, and the saving of time and of money can scarcely compensate for so serious a drawback. But unfortunately in these fast days of ours, when everything is done in a hurry, and every man seems to run a race against time, the steamer is in general demand, and the journey by dahabiah has become a *royage de luxe*. So much the worse for Egypt, which cannot be done justice to in a visit " à la vapeur."

The antiquities which may be seen from the banks of the Nile, or which are described in the guide-books, are very numerous. We will only stop at those of real archæological interest, and with which it is indispensable for the traveller to become acquainted.

I.—BENI-HASSAN.

	Miles
From Boolák to Bedrechyn	15
,, Bedrechyn to Zawyet	41
,, Zawyet to Beni-Souef	19
,, Beni-Souef to Fechn	22

		Miles
From Fechn to Abou-Girgeh	...	31
,, Abou-Girgeh to Kolosaneh	...	13
,, Kolosaneh to Minieh ...	...	23
,, Minieh to Beni-Hassan	...	15
From Boolák to Beni-Hassan	...	179

From Boolák to Beni-Souef the route is rather wearisome. The banks of the river are low, the landscape is monotonous, and the villages fall flat on the eye. A strangely shaped pyramid attracts the traveller's attention for many hours on the way. This is the Pyramid of Meydoum, which from a distance seems to stand on the top of a hillock. This hillock, however, is nothing but an artificial mound formed by the crumbling away of the outer casing. The Arabs call it *Haram-el-Katdab* (the false pyramid); for they suppose it to be formed of the rock itself, to which a rough sort of masonry has given the shape of a pyramid, an assertion we are not in a position to verify, as the pyramid has never been opened.

Be this as it may, the Pyramid of Meydoum is certainly the most carefully constructed and the best-built pyramid in Egypt. What we see of it now is doubtless only its nucleus, and when complete (if ever it was complete), it was, perhaps, built in steps like the greater number of the monuments of this kind. The name of the king who caused it to be constructed for his own tomb is unknown; there is, however, some reason to suppose that it was Snefrou, the predecessor of Cheops. Around the pyramid extends the necropolis, which mostly belongs to the time of the first of these two Pharaohs. It was in the chamber of the most northern *mastabah* of this necropolis that we discovered, in January 1872, the two admirable statues which are now in the jewel-room of the Boolák Museum.

From Beni-Souef the scenery becomes rather more animated, and one begins to perceive, standing out from the horizon, the innumerable chimneys of the sugar-factories of the Khedive, which promise so much prosperity and riches for Egypt at no distant time. A little beyond Kolosaneh, we pass at the foot of the mountain of Gebel-Teir (the mountain of birds). There, on a rocky eminence, stands the convent of Deir--el-Bakarah, so called on account of the pulley by which travellers formerly gained access into its interior. It is inhabited by monks, who profess to be shoemakers by trade, but whose principal occupation would seem to be to precipitate themselves into the water as soon as they perceive the approach of a dahabiah or a steamer, and, having forced themselves on board, to solicit alms, in a scantiness of costume of the impropriety of which they themselves seem to be utterly unconscious. The convent is rich, and travellers would do well to drive away these importunate beggars, who, when there is but little wind, often cause much annoyance by their audacious obstinacy.

Beyond Minieh, the Arabian chain opens itself to view along the banks of the river, in fairly regular horizontal lines. With the assistance of a field-glass, one may soon discern hollowed out in the side of the mountain, about one-third of the way from the summit, some tombs preceded by columns. These are the grotto tombs of Beni--Hassan, situated about two miles from the halting-place of the boats. They are not all of equal interest, the most remarkable being the two last to the north. These grottoes are tombs of the early part of the XIIth dynasty (3,000 years B.C.). The personages buried here were, in their lifetime, public functionaries in the city to which this mountain once served as a burial-place, but of which we know neither the name nor the exact site.

The Beni-Hassan tombs are constructed on the same principle as those with which we are already acquainted at the Pyramids and at Sakkârah. They consist of: 1st, an accessible chamber which at Sakkârah and at the Pyramids is inclosed within the mass of the mastabah, but which here is hollowed in the rock; 2nd, a well carefully hidden and blocked up, leading down to the vault (here the opening of the well is found in the centre, or in one of the corners of the chamber); 3rd, a funeral vault where the sarcophagus and the mummy were deposited, and which is situated alike at the Pyramids, at Sakkârah and at Beni-Hassan, at the bottom of the well. The style of the decoration is also similar, only the scenes have undergone a slight change. More than ever, the deceased is seen in his home. Still more details are given bearing upon his biography and the various scenes and incidents of his life. He is hunting wild animals in the desert; captives bring him gifts; acrobats execute in his presence various gymnastic feats. Moreover, as a characteristic sign alike of the Ancient and of the Middle Empire, there is the same absence of all representation of the divinity.

As we have already said, the most important of the Beni-Hassan tombs are the two situated immediately to the north. Architects will undoubtedly find much to admire in their style, and it is well emphatically to remind the reader that the magnificent columns which adorn the frontage of both these tombs, and also the interior of one of them, have preceded our Christian era, notwithstanding their Doric appearance, by some three thousand years.

The first tomb to the north is that of *Ameni--Amenemha* (thus called after a king of the XIth dynasty who bore these two names). In the inscription which covers both sides of the entrance doorway, Ameni-Amenemha relates the history of his life. He was general of infantry, and in that capacity had led one campaign against the *Apou*, and another against the Ethiopians. The king who reigned at the time was Usertasen I. It was with the son of this king that Ameni--Amenemha marched to battle. He was also governor of the province of *Sah*, and in that capacity he merited the approbation of his sovereign by his good administration, &c. &c.

The second tomb is that of *Noum-Hotep*. The paintings therein are admirable, although they have suffered much from age, and have fared still worse at the hands of those travellers who seem to think that the greater is the value which attaches to a monument, the more tempting it is to take away from that value by engraving their names thereon. The tomb of Noum-Hotep dates, like that of Ameni-Amenemha, from the commencement of the XIIth dynasty, but it belongs to the reign of Amenemha II. In the long inscription which encircles the sub-basement of the chamber, Noum-Hotep also relates the history of his life. His father and mother and ancestors were established in the town of *Menat-Koufou* (possibly Minich). His father had resided there as a state official and a governor of the eastern provinces. He himself was, like Ameni--Amenemha, governor of the district of Sah. Then follows the enumeration of his good deeds. He has honoured the gods, he has caused the temples to overflow with his gifts, and so forth.

In the northern wall of the tomb of Noum--Hotep, a remarkably curious scene is represented, which unfortunately is gradually fading away from day to day. Noum-Hotep is standing.

Personages with a strongly marked aquiline nose, and a black and pointed beard, are ushered into his presence, accompanied by their wives and children. They advance, followed by their asses and by antelopes and wild goats, which are probably all the cattle they possess. Some among them carry arms (arrows, pikes, clubs), and one of the number is playing a sort of lyre. An inscription explains the meaning of this picture. These are thirty-seven *Amou*, who present themselves before Noum-Hotep, and in token of submission offer him the precious aromatic called Nest'em. This episode in the life of Noum-Hotep doubtless possesses in itself but a secondary interest, yet it deserves attention from its being the most ancient known example of those immigrations of an Asiatic race which later on played so important a part in the affairs of Egypt. The word *Amou* means literally *shepherd*, or *cowherd*, and is the generic name of the Syro-Aramaic races. These Amou of Noum--Hotep are in fact the first instalment of the immigrating hordes who were in all ages attracted by the proverbial fertility of Egypt, and settled in the eastern portion of the Delta. The Jews were eventually to be included in the Amou, together with other nations; and if the testimony afforded by the monuments of Sân can sufficiently be relied on when estimated by the standard of such of the Amou as are still to be found in Egypt, the name of Amou may fairly be given also to the Shepherd-Kings. Indeed, the much dreaded inhabitants of the marshes spoken of by historians are none other than Amou who had settled in Egypt. In their out-of-the-way *Bucholics*, where they had settled down, they afforded shelter to Psammetichus and to Amyrtœus. Later on, under the name of *Bi-Amites* (*Bi* here represents the article in Egyptian), they gave themselves up to brigandage, and cut to pieces the troops of the Kaliphs Merwan and Mamoun that had been sent against them. Lastly, we may recognise the descendants of the same Amou in the present inhabitants of Lake Menzaleh, and of part of the eastern district of the Delta, who live by their fisheries and their flocks, and who, until lately, relying on their quality as foreigners, obstinately refused to pay certain taxes. The Amou, therefore, of the Noum-Hotep picture, whatever may have been their tribe, boast a history. After a lapse of 4,800 years, they stand before us as the first foreign people who yielded to that fascinating attraction of the land of Egypt, the traces of which have not yet altogether disappeared.

II.—ABYDOS.

	Miles
From Beni-Hassan to Rhodah	12
,, Rhodah to Melawi	7½
,, Melawi to Haggi-Kandil	7
,, Haggi-Kandil to Gebel-abou-Fedah	18
,, Gebel-abou-Fedah to Manfalout	11½
,, Manfalout to Siout	27
,, Siout to Aboutig	17
,, Aboutig to Tahtah	28½
,, Tahtah to Sohag	27
,, Sohag to Menshieh	12
,, Menshieh to Girgeh	13
,, Girgeh to Bellianeh	8
From Beni-Hassan to Bellianeh	188½

From Boolák to Bellianeh, 367½ miles.

From Beni-Hassan to Bellianeh (Abydos) the route is long and somewhat monotonous.

The first halting-place is Rhodah, where the tourist may visit the magnificent factory founded by his highness the Khedive.

The traveller who has a day to spare might make good use of it in visiting the grottoes of

Tel-Amarna, and Haggi-Kandil would then be chosen as a landing-place. The grottoes of Tel--Amarna belong to the XVIIIth dynasty, and to that still obscure period when, under a king who probably laboured under monomania, the Egyptian religion suddenly degenerated into a schism. If these tombs were not situated so far from the river, and at the same time at such a distance one from the other, they would certainly be more frequently visited, as indeed they deserve to be. They are, with but few exceptions, the tombs of officials of the court of Amenophis IV. (the *Khou-en-Aten* of the monuments), and of two or three of his immediate successors. The personages here represented are remarkably portly and corpulent. A fashion has been introduced in funeral matters under Amenophis IV., which will prevail again during the reign of Rameses II. Under both these princes the artists have apparently made it a point of honour to give the figures they executed the very features of the reigning king; and it is out of compliment to their sovereign that the individuals buried in Tel-Amarna display those eunuch-looking heads and those forms overladen with fat, which impart so strange an aspect to the bas-reliefs of this necropolis.

Gebel-abou-Fedah is the name given to the precipitous chain of mountains which, a little before reaching Manfalout, rise so abruptly from the river. High up in these mountains, almost at their southernmost extremity, are the famous grottoes of Maabdeh. Access is obtained to them through a natural fissure in the rock, as a house would be entered by the roof, and one finds oneself in a spot literally filled with mummies of crocodiles. But little explored at present, these mysterious caves have probably much to reveal to us, for no one knows how far they extend either to the right or to the left. With those mummies of crocodiles are found intermingled some human mummies, the richest of which are gilded from head to foot, whilst even the poorest can boast of some sort of decoration in the form of square-shaped leaves of gold placed in immediate contact with the skin. One may well wonder, in penetrating into the caves of Maabdeh, whence could come these thousands and thousands of crocodiles which lie in heaps one over the other. For now-a-days, it is the rarest possible thing to see even one or two of these reptiles during a voyage on the Nile. The answer is a simple one. In the first place, but a short while ago crocodiles were much more frequently seen than they are now; moreover, the mountain of Gebel-abou-Fedah was always one of their favourite resorts. Let the traveller watch carefully the fissures of the rocks which lie closest to the water's edge. Very frequently what at first sight appears to be nothing but a log of wood lying against the rock, proves to be a crocodile with extended jaws basking in the sun. Now, if the description we have given of the tomb of Tih (page 98) is not already forgotten by the reader, it will be seen that not only the crocodile, but even the hippopotamus also formerly existed close to Memphis, *i.e.* almost as low down as Cairo; it is evident, therefore, that these animals must formerly have been found on the Nile in far greater numbers than at present. Moreover, let it be borne in mind that in the days of Abd-el-Latyf (1190 of the present era) hippopotami were still to be found in the Damietta branch. Therefore, seeing what a number of crocodile-mummies are found, not only at Maabdeh, but also in various other parts of Egypt, one may rest assured that once upon a time the Nile produced these creatures in considerable numbers. When Champollion passed Keneh, he saw fourteen crocodiles "in solemn conclave" on an islet. If the like good fortune never now falls to the lot of the tourist, it is because the crocodile is driven back farther and farther south by the fire-arms of travellers, and the constant passing of steamboats, to such an extent that the Nile is likely ere long to know them no more below Assouán, except by tradition.

Manfalout, Siout,* Tahtah, Sohag and Girgeh are passed one after the other in rapid succession, and have but little to recommend them to the antiquarian. For those who wish to visit Abydos, the next halting-place would be Bellianeh. Formerly Abydos was reached from Girgeh, the route lying along the dyke as far as the desert, a distance of twelve to thirteen miles, but now the road from Bellianeh saves half the distance.

At Abydos are to be seen the *Temple of Sethi*, the *Temple of Rameses*, the *Tomb of Osiris*, and the *Necropolis*.

* Siout, however, deserves a visit, being the capital of the province, and having an important trade with Darfur, from whence caravans arrive periodically. Its pottery works are justly renowned. It is a picturesque place, and the bazaars afford many interesting studies, both of costume and manners.

The temple of Sethi is the first temple which is visited in Upper Egypt. In order thoroughly to understand the meaning of the numerous pictures which adorn its walls, the reader is recommended to refer to the explanations given in the first pages of this volume. The king who founded the temple is in the presence of one or more divinities; such is, nine times out of ten, the *motif* of each one of the pictures which form the decoration of the temple. The temple of Sethi is the *Memnonium* of Strabo, deservedly famous for the magnificence of its sculptures. It was founded by Sethi I., the father of Rameses II. All that bears the name of this prince is remarkable for the artistic manner of its treatment; while on the contrary the sculptures of Rameses are poor, and too often of a most indifferent workmanship. The temple of Sethi, moreover, is one of the edifices of Egypt the purport and meaning of which are most difficult to grasp. Properly speaking, it is composed of seven naves or bays, leading into seven sanctuaries, as if dedicated to seven different deities. The southernmost aisle, which is joined on in such an irregular manner to the principal building, constitutes another problem difficult of solution. Then again, both its founders, the kings Sethi and Rameses, are represented in company one with the other in such a fashion that we must inevitably conclude that these two kings reigned conjointly; or, in other terms, that the temple was in course of construction when the father associated his son with him on the throne. By way of information we may add that it was in the temple of Sethi that we discovered a chronological table of kings, more complete and in a better state of preservation than that which has enriched the collection of the British Museum (see the ascending passage to the south of the second Hall of Columns). Sethi as king, and Rameses still as a prince, are there represented standing; the one offering the sacrifice of fire, the other reciting the sacred hymn. Before them, as in a sort of synoptical diagram, are the cartouches of the seventy-six kings (Sethi has included himself among the number), to whom this homage is paid, and it is not without a certain emotion that one reads at the head of the proud list the name of Menes, the ancient and venerable founder of the Egyptian monarchy.*

A little to the north of the temple of Sethi

* For a description of the vaulted chambers, see page 38.

is that of Rameses II. Of the latter, however, nothing remains but the walls to a height of scarcely five feet ; nor have the excavations that have been carried on here enabled us to draw out a complete plan of this temple, from which the " Tablet of Abydos " at the British Museum was carried away — a mutilated copy of the table we found entire in the temple of Sethi. It is easily understood that a temple so completely devastated as the one we are at present contemplating should throw but little light on the question of mythology. But the question of origin is by no means so obscure, and we know for certain that the temple of Rameses II. is contemporary with the Paris obelisk, that is to say, it was begun by Rameses II. when he was associated with his father on the throne, and was completed by him after he had become sole monarch.

Still proceeding towards the north, we come upon a large encircling wall of crude brick. This is the ancient site of Thinis, the cradle of the Egyptian monarchy; here also stood the tomb of the Osiris of Abydos, which was to the inhabitants of Egypt what the Holy Sepulchre is to Christians. Unfortunately there now remains absolutely nothing of Egypt's most ancient and most venerated sanctuary, nor is there the faintest hope that even the foundations will ever be brought to light by any fresh excavations. Close by, however, and also comprised within the enceinte, is a tumulus, from which one is justified in expecting great results. This is the *Kom-es-Sultan*. The Kom-es-Sultan is not a natural mound; it is the result of the constant accumulation of tombs which have thus been heaped up one over the other, through successive generations. According to Plutarch, the wealthy inhabitants were brought from all parts of Egypt to be interred at Abydos, in order that they might repose close to Osiris. In all probability, the tombs of Kom-es-Sultan belong to the personages of whom Plutarch speaks. The only interest that this tumulus of Kom-es-Sultan possesses is that there can be no doubt the famous tomb of Osiris is not far off, and certain indications would lead one to believe that it is hollowed out of the self-same rock which serves as the basis of this mound, so that the personages interred there repose as near as possible to the last resting-place of their beloved Osiris.

The excavations now being carried on at Kom--es-Sultan have therefore a double interest: they may furnish us with valuable tombs which become more and more ancient the further we penetrate into the sides of the mountain, so that it is not unreasonable to hope that in time we may come upon some belonging even to the Ist dynasty. In the second place, they may any day lead us to the discovery of the still unknown entrance of the divine tomb, if indeed it were ever a subterranean vault.

As for the necropolis itself, however much interest it may have afforded during our excavations (and it furnished the greater part of the valuable collection of stelæ which is to be seen at the Boolák Museum), its appearance has been so entirely changed by those excavations, that it has lost much of its attraction for the ordinary traveller. Let us state, in conclusion, that the tombs of the necropolis of Abydos belong principally to the VIth dynasty (3700 years B.C.), to the XIIth dynasty (3000 years B.C.), and to the XIIIth dynasty (2800 years B.C.) We may further notice that the greater number of the tombs of the XIIIth dynasty consist of pyramids economically built of crude bricks, the interior being hollowed out in the form of a cupola; and again, that it is not at all unusual, among the tombs of this period, as also of the VIth dynasty, to find vaulted roofs which take the form of a pointed arch, and where, moreover, the bricks of the ogive are wedge-shaped.

III.—DENDERAH.

	Miles
From Bellianeh to Farschout	20
,, Farschout to Kasr-es-sayad ...	8
,, Kasr-es-sayad to Keneh... ...	30
From Bellianeh to Keneh	58

From Boolák to Keneh, 425½ miles.

Between Bellianeh and Keneh there is no place particularly deserving of the traveller's attention, but Farschout has an industrial establishment of great importance. Tombs of the VIth dynasty are to be seen at Kasr-es-sayad. Some of the rock tombs of this locality are covered with numberless Coptic inscriptions which are worth studying. Keneh is with Siout, Esneh and Assouán, one of the modern towns of Upper Egypt which travellers usually visit.

Keneh is situated on the right bank of the river; and almost immediately opposite, on the left bank, is the temple of Denderah. This is one of the best preserved and the most important of Egypt's temples. It was built, like all Egyptian temples, in the centre of a vast encircling wall of crude bricks, which was so high and so thick that when the two gates were closed through which admission was obtained, nothing could be seen or heard of what was taking place inside. The history of the temple of Denderah may be summed up in a few words. Its foundations were laid under Ptolemy XI.; its construction was finished under Tiberius, and its decoration under Nero. Jesus Christ was living at Jerusalem when this temple was being completed.

No one can fail to be struck with the profusion of inscriptions, of pictures and of bas-reliefs with which it is covered. Even the ceilings, the doors, the windows, the basement, and the walls of the staircases are crowded in every part. It is true the composition of these many pictures is the same throughout. The king presents himself before one of the divinities of the temple and recites a prayer; he solicits a favour which is always granted; this is the inevitable subject.

A stranger standing in the midst of the temple of Denderah cannot help wondering what could be the intention of this vast assemblage of buildings. This we will try to explain.

According to the purpose for which they were intended, the chambers of the temple of Denderah may be divided into four groups, as follows :

1. The first group consists only of the hall A (see the accompanying plan). The hall A is merely a sort of monumental frontage. Open to the light of day, and exposed to all external sounds, it has no direct relationship with the temple properly so called. Two small doors are let in at the sides. Through these doors the priests passed to and fro, and the offerings were brought in which played so important a part in the innermost service of the temple. Through the large portal the king alone had the right to pass. The king presented himself before it, clothed in his long robe, wearing sandals on his feet and leaning on his staff. Before he could be allowed to penetrate into the temple it was necessary that the gods should recognise him as king of Upper and of Lower Egypt, and it is to the ceremonies commemorating this consecration that the first pictures to the right and to the left of the entrance gate are dedicated. There we see the king coming out of his palace and presenting himself before the gate of the

temple. To the right, *i.e* on the northern side, he is recognised as king of Lower Egypt; to the left, *i.e.* on the southern side, he is entitled king of Upper Egypt. On his arrival, Thoth and Horus pour over his head the emblems of purification. The goddesses Ouat'i and Suvan crown him with the double crown. After which Mont of Thebes and Toum of Heliopolis take the king by the hand, and conduct him into the presence of the goddess Hathor.* Thus the hall A is only an entrance, a place of passage. Here it is that the king prepares himself for those ceremonies which we shall see him celebrating in the interior of the edifice.

2. The second group is composed of the chambers B, C, D, E, F, G, H, I, J and K. We are now in the temple properly so called. Here all is closely shut in, all is sombre, all is silent. It was in these ten chambers of the second group that the priests assembled, and that the preparations for the fêtes were carried on. A sort of calendar engraved on the walls of the hall B tells us what was the nature of these fêtes. They consisted mostly in processions which went round the temple, ascended the

* For a further description of these pictures, see p. 40.

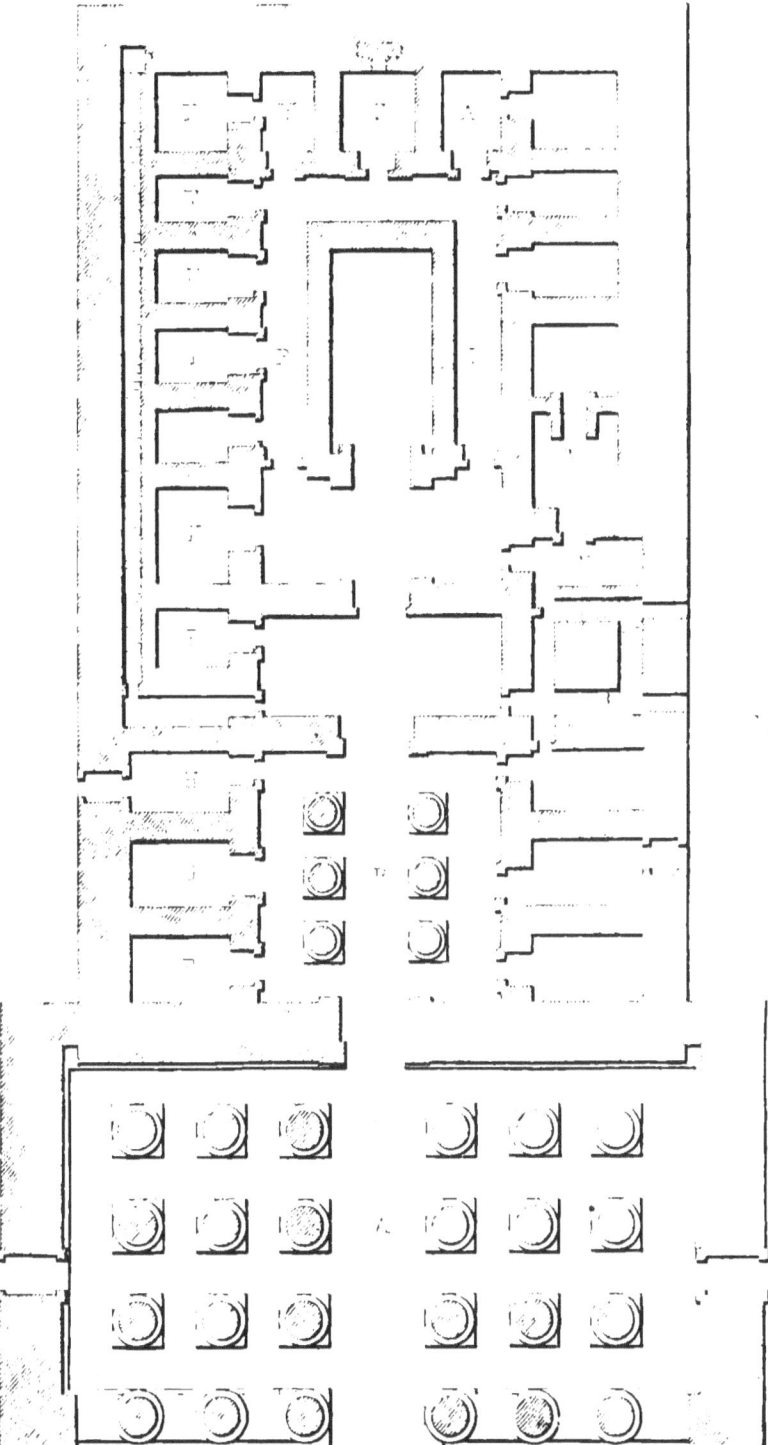

terraces, and descended again in order to encompass the encircling wall, according to the prescribed rites. Now it was from the hall B that these processions started. The other chambers served for the preparation of the offerings destined to figure in the fêtes, and also as a place where the sacred emblems, carried in state during the processions, were deposited and carefully preserved. The halls C and D were annexes of the hall B, and contained altars before which certain prayers were recited as the procession passed. In the hall E were kept the four barks which played so conspicuous a part in the processions. When not in use these barks were placed upon large chests, and when required for the service of the temple staves of wood were adjusted into them, by means of which they were carried about. In the centre of each of these barks was a small edifice, always securely closed, wherein lay placed the mystic emblem of the particular divinity to whom the bark was dedicated. By way of additional precaution, a thick white veil was thrown over this structure which was thus completely hidden from all eyes. (Compare with this the description of the ark in the Bible.) The chamber F is a laboratory, in which were prepared the oils and essences with which the temple and the statues of the gods were to be perfumed. In the chamber G were collected together and consecrated such products of the earth as were to be introduced in the ceremonies. The chambers H and I served as places of reception, the one for the offerings arriving from Lower Egypt, the other for those from Upper Egypt; and here also were received and consecrated certain offerings of loaves of bread and of libations. The chamber J was the treasury of the temple, and this is why each of the pictures with which its walls are lined exhibits to us the king in the act of consecrating and offering to the divinity sistra, pectorals, mirrors, utensils of all sorts fashioned with gold and silver and lapis-lazuli. In chamber K were deposited the vestments with which they draped the statues of the gods. Coffers scrupulously closed contained these vestments, and each province of Egypt was expected to contribute to the keeping up of the sacred stores in chamber K.

3. The third group contains the chapel L, the court M, the halls N, O, P, Q, the two flights of stairs, the one to the north, the other to the south, and lastly the little temple with twelve

columns situated on the terraces, and which we cannot introduce into our plan. The principal fête of the temple, that which is celebrated on the first day of the year, and which has for its object the first appearance of the star Sirius, is of such vast importance that at Denderah a smaller temple has been dedicated to it, inclosed as it were inside the larger temple, and it is this smaller temple that is composed of the various parts which we have been enumerating. Prayers were recited in the chapel L. In the court M the various offerings were collected together, as also were the different limbs of the victims slaughtered for the sacrifice. The little chamber N was another place of deposit for the many valuable objects which were brought forth in this special fête. In the three chambers O, P and Q, the king consecrated certain offerings. Like the other fêtes of the temple, that of the new year consisted chiefly in processions, the details of which will be found on the walls of both the flights of stairs. The king marches at the head; thirteen priests carrying standard poles crowned with the emblems of different divinities follow him, and so forth; thus constituted, the procession ascended by the northern staircase, stopped on the terrace at the hypæthral temple, the twelve columns of which are dedicated each to a particular month of the year, and descended by the southern staircase.

4. The fourth group comprises the corridor R,* the chambers S, T, U, V, X, Y, Z, A', B', C' and D'. This part of the edifice is more particularly reserved to the myth, and here was to be found the nucleus of the whole, a niche situated in the chamber Z. Here the king alone could penetrate; here, hidden from all eyes, was the mysterious emblem of the temple, a large sistrum of gold. The chambers themselves were not set apart for any distinct purpose, as were the others, although in them were preserved various objects connected with the religious rites, but they served more especially for the recital of prayers. In the chamber S it is Isis who is invoked. The chamber T is consecrated to Osiris. Here Osiris is supposed to be recalled from death to life, which was symbolised in this chamber by changing the vestments that covered the statue of the god. The chamber U was sacred to Osiris-Onnophris. Here the god restores

* We have already described, at page 85, a part of the corridor R.

youth to his body, imparts fresh vigour to his limbs, and forthwith comes before us as the vanquisher of his enemies represented by a crocodile, which the god, armed with a pike, "drives backwards." In the chamber V the work of resurrection is completed, and the god appears under the form of Hor-sam-ta-ui. In the chambers X and Y, it is Hathor who is worshipped, taken in her attributes of divine genitrix, out of whom the Sun daily takes his renewed birth. The chamber Z is in the axis of the temple, and the principal divinity is there adored under the most comprehensive titles. Lastly, in the chambers A', B', C', D', a special worship is paid to Pascht, considered as the fire that vivifies; to Horus, considered as the light which has conquered darkness, and to the terrestrial Hathor.

Such is the temple properly so called, which therefore is not, like our churches, a place where the faithful meet together to unite in prayer. We find neither dwellings for the priests, nor any place of initiation, nor traces of oracle or divination; nor is there anything to indicate that with the exception of the king and the priests any person was ever permitted to enter here. The temple was a sacred depository, a place of preparation and of consecration. Within its walls certain fêtes were celebrated and processions organised, and the sacred vessels carefully stored away; if inside all was dark and sombre—and nothing whatever indicates the use of torches or any other artificial light—that darkness was intended to intensify the mystery of the ceremonies, while at the same time it secured the only mode known of preserving the precious objects and the sacred vestments from the ravages of insects, from flies, from the penetrating dust, and from the scorching sun. As to the principal fêtes of which the temple was at once the centre and the starting-point, they consisted chiefly in processions which were carried on outside in the full sunshine, as far as the extreme boundary of the great encircling wall of crude bricks. In short, the temple was not entirely contained within its stone walls, its true limits being rather those of the enceinte. In the temple itself the gods were housed and draped and prepared for the fêtes; it was in fact a sort of sacristy where none but the king or the priests might enter. But within the encircling wall long processions were organised, and if the general public were not admitted, we may at least believe that some few initiated were privileged to take part in these processions. We may add that the numerous Coptic and Arab dwellings which have invaded the whole circumference of the temple, and even of the enceinte itself, no longer permit of our fully realising what this temple might once have been, when it arose stately and isolated, the centre of a vast area shut in at the four corners of heaven by high and sombre walls of crude brick.

There is another part of the temple of which as yet we have said nothing, but which travellers are in the habit of visiting—we mean the crypts. These are long, narrow, secret corridors intercolated into the thickness of the foundations and of the inner walls of the temple. It must have been the intention of the architect to make of these crypts secret hiding-places; they had neither doors, nor windows, nor opening of any sort, and when they were entered it was only by some special mechanism that the stone which mysteriously blocked up the entrance could be removed. For what purpose could those crypts have been intended? There can be no doubt as to the actual use to which they were put. Statues of the divinities in gold, in silver, in lapis-lazuli, and in wood were secreted there, as also sistra and jewelled collars and emblems of all kinds; and on certain fête-days these were fetched away, that they might be carried in state in the processions. Except on the rare occasions when these sacred objects were thus brought out to lend their aid to the embellishment of the religious ceremonies the crypts were so securely closed that from the inner chambers of the temple their existence would never for a moment have been suspected. But if we may be content with this explanation of the use to which these crypts were put, it is by no means so easy to determine for what specific purpose they were originally constructed. Numberless inscriptions cover the walls; unfortunately, however, minute as are the details which these inscriptions afford us respecting the dimensions of the objects therein contained, their numbers and the material of which they are composed, these same inscriptions are trivial and utterly devoid of interest upon all other points. Notwithstanding all one's efforts, it is therefore impossible to make the crypts tell their own tale as to their relationship to the temple. One can only imagine that the construction of those corridors hidden underground bears a certain analogy to the ideas, so abundantly illustrated throughout the temple, of burial and of resurrection, of life latent and life active, of germination unseen and the efflorescence that ensues.

The terraces also will be found interesting. We have already made acquaintance with the little temple of twelve columns. There are six other chambers equally worthy of notice. These six chambers are divided into two groups of three chambers each, one group to the north, the other to the south; and the two groups form together a small temple which is dedicated to Osiris.

According to the invariable tradition, both of the monuments and of classical writers, Osiris is always described as the universal god of the Egyptians. Egypt was divided into forty-two provinces or nomes, and each of these forty-two nomes possessed a local Osiris, so that, correctly speaking, Egypt recognised forty-two different forms of Osiris. Now the deity of the small temple on the terrace is the Osiris of the nome of Denderah, worshipped under the name of *Osiris-An*.

As to the little temple being divided into two groups of chambers, the one to the north, the other to the south, it was on account of the local deities of the same name which the Osiris of Denderah admitted by his side as secondary divinities. On the northern side were the Osiris of the northern nomes, whilst the Osiris of the southern provinces had access to the southern chambers. This explanation will afford a clue to the particular purpose for which the little temple of the terraces was constructed. Osiris, and more particularly the Osiris of Denderah, was there worshipped; but in thus becoming a local divinity the Osiris of Denderah lost none of the qualities of the principal Osiris; and what we see on the walls of the little temple refers chiefly to the Osiris of the national traditions, that is to say, to the Osiris who came down upon earth as the benefactor of mankind, who was put to death, and who rose again. We here become acquainted with the forty-two names of Osiris in the forty-two nomes.* We find long processions of the gods carrying in vases the members of Osiris which each town possesses.† In

* Frieze of the second chamber to the S.

† Second room to the S. In this chamber was formerly the planisphere or zodiac which is now in Paris; the traces of its removal may still be seen. The astronomical representations sculptured on the ceiling of four of the chambers of the little temple have no direct relationship

another place the forty-two funeral biers of Osiris are represented.* Then come the twelve hours of the day, with a notice of the prayers to be said at each hour; and also the twelve hours of the night, the whole being divided after the same manner as the temple itself into Upper and Lower Egypt.† As to the fêtes, this time they consist of processions in which priests from all parts of Egypt take part.‡ A calendar sets forth all the details,§ while it gives recipes for the preparation of the oils, the perfumes and the essences which should be used. Short notices furnish also the calendar of these same fêtes for the Osiris of the other towns.

Considered with reference to the dogma which it represents, the temple of Denderah bears the

with the myth to which this edifice is dedicated. The heavens are there vaguely portrayed as they were conceived by the Egyptians, together with the divine forms that are supposed to dwell there. Astronomy, as a science, is not in any way treated of, and we find neither an original scheme nor a projection of the heavens calculated upon any precise standing-point.

* Third room to the S., and third room to the N.
† Second room to the S., and second room to the N.
‡ Sub-basement at the entrance of the first chamber to the S.
§ See the long texts engraved on the side walls of the southern chamber.

stamp of a philosophical spirit which cannot fail to awaken the highest interest. The principal divinity of the temple is Hathor, the Aphrodite or Venus of classical tradition. In her principal character Hathor is the pupil of the Sun's eye, and thus the Egyptians made Hathor the goddess of beauty, the seat of which they placed chiefly in the eyes. Then come her other titles —the goddess of the lovely face, the beautiful goddess, the goddess of love. At the same time Hathor is represented as the personification of the general harmony of the world, which exists and endures only through the harmonious cooperation of all its parts. Thus she is the divine mother who causes all vegetation to germinate, who makes the corn to grow, who gives life to mortals, who carries fecundity and abundance into all parts of the world, love being productive only in such measure as it is harmonious. Again, one of the characters under which the inscriptions of the temple most frequently represent Hathor is that which connects her with every idea of youthfulness, of expansion, and of resurrection; this is exemplified even in the subjects chosen for the decoration of the frieze, and of the sub-basement, where flowers in blossom, stems of plants crossing each other and intertwining, scarabæi alternating with the phœnix, shadow forth at every step the eternal beauty of nature. It is even as a symbol of these ideas of constant renovation that Hathor is so frequently designated the goddess Sothis (Sirius), Hathor thus becomes the star which determines and governs the periodical return of the year,* which announces the rising of the river; she is the star whose appearance at the eastern horizon at the same moment as the rising sun foretells the renewal of nature. Hathor then, like the Aphrodite of the Greeks, is something more than the goddess of beauty; the Hathor of the Egyptians is the type of that universal harmony which is necessary to the well-being and to the life of the world; what they desired to personify in her was the ideal of all that is beautiful.

Perhaps if the temple of Denderah were of Pharaonic origin, and consequently free from all Grecian influence, the inscriptions would carry us no farther. But from the arrangements of

* The Egyptian year commenced on the 21st July, the day when Sothis and the Sun appear simultaneously in the morning horizon.

certain pictures, invariably placed opposite each entrance door, and where the king himself is represented as offering to the Divinity a statuette of truth,* Hathor is evidently intended to personify not only the goddess of all that is beautiful, but also the goddess of all that is true. According to custom, inscriptions accompany these pictures. In front of the king are the words he is supposed to pronounce; in front of the goddess is the answer which she is supposed to make to the king's speech. In all the chambers, with the exception of the sanctuary, the speech is meaningless enough on either side: "I offer to thee Truth," says the king; "I raise her towards thee, O Hathor, sovereign lady of the Heavens." The goddess replies, "May Truth be with thee, mayest thou live by her, and by her means triumph over thine enemies (*i.e.* may falsehood ever be vanquished by truth)!" But in the sanctuary the triviality of these texts disappears, and in entering the chamber the king exclaims, "I offer to thee Truth, O goddess of

---

* Truth is represented by a little statue of a female seated in a basket, her head crowned with a waving feather. The king holds the basket in his outstretched hand, and presents it to the goddess who stands before him.

Denderah, for Truth is thine own work, for thou art Truth itself." The philosophical character of Hathor is thus more and more forcibly illustrated.

A third attribute of Hathor, no less characteristic than the two former, is clearly manifested by the care that has been taken to assign to her an especial place in the temple of the terraces. Here she is no longer the same Hathor that we have known below; she is transformed into Isis, she becomes the goddess who attaches herself to Osiris, who accompanies him from chamber to chamber, and who is present at his resurrection. Now Osiris, according to the tradition handed down to us by Plutarch, is the principle of good. "Osiris," says Plutarch, "takes pleasure in doing good, and his name, amongst many other meanings, is said to express activity and beneficence." Again, Plutarch shows us Isis and Osiris, sometimes governing the kingdom of good, sometimes presiding over intellect, the principle of all good. "Isis," says Plutarch, "possesses an innate love of good principles." Moreover, without going so far as the terraces for an illustration, does not the interior of the temple impress us with the same idea, when we notice that among the nine emblems of the temple the foremost rank has been ascribed to the sistrum? "The sistrum," says Plutarch, "symbolises that men should always be active and busy; that they must be constantly stimulated and roused out of the state of languor and enervation into which they are too prone to fall. It is said that the sound of this instrument puts Typhon to flight." Death vanquished to the benefit of life; evil suppressed to the benefit of good; falsehood dissipated by truth: this then is the symbol of which the sistrum is the genuine type, and by this one sees that to the same ideas of universal harmony, that is to say, of the beautiful and the true, which we found so ingeniously applied in the interior of the temple, is here added the idea of good.

The temple of Denderah therefore presents a certain arrangement which no doubt would never be displayed by a temple of Pharaonic origin, and this it is which betrays the influence of the times in which it was erected. Evidently the Platonic schools of thought then flourishing at Alexandria extended their influence as far as Denderah, and the entire decoration of the temple is composed with a view to summing up synthetically, under the imagery of local divinities and their attributes, the three fundamental parts of that philosophy, the Beautiful, the True, and the Good.

IV.—THEBES.

	Miles
From Keneh to Naggadeh	22½
,, Naggadeh to Luxor	16
From Keneh to Luxor	38½

From Boolák to Luxor, 464 miles.

Thebes spreads itself on both banks of the Nile, just as London and Paris extend over both banks of the Thames and Seine.

On the right bank are the temples of *Karnak* and of *Luxor*. On the left bank, going from N. to S., are the temple of *Goornah*, the temple of *Deir-el-Bahari*, the *Rameseum*, the *Colossi*, the temple of *Deir-el-Medineh*, and the temple of *Medinet-Abou*. Besides these there were other temples which adorned the left side of Thebes; but they are utterly demolished, and some among them have hardly left any traces by which their site may be ascertained. On the left bank are also to be found the various cemeteries of Thebes. Behind the temple of Goornah is that which is called *Drah-Abou'l-neggah*. In front of Deir-el--Bahari is a second necropolis called *El-Assassif*, and on the slope of the hills situated behind the Ramescum is another called *Scheikh Abd-el--Goornah*, and *Goornah-Mouraï*. We may further mention the *Valley of Queens* and the two *Valleys of Kings* (*Bab-el-Molouk*), situated in the desert at some little distance to the west.

Thinis (Abydos) and Memphis are the two most ancient capitals of Egypt, being cotemporaneous with the foundation of the Egyptian monarchy. Thebes makes her first appearance in history with the kings of the XIth dynasty. This is one of the most curious periods that the antiquarian can study. If we may believe the testimony of the monuments, Egypt was just recovering, either from an invasion or from long ages of internal troubles which had lasted since the end of the VI$_{th}$ dynasty. All at once, the broken links in the chain of tradition are restored, and Thebes appears with a civilisation of her own, as shown by the tombs of that remote period—a civilisation which differs widely from that which may be studied at Sakkárah, at Meydoum, at Zawyet-el-Maïtin, at Kasr-es--Sayad, on the latest monuments of the VIth dynasty. The manner in which the mummies are arranged, the style of the hieroglyphs, the formulas employed, all seems changed. The inhabitants of Thebes interred at *Drah-abou'l--neggah*, the necropolis of that early period, were frequently negroes. The coffins are formed of the hollowed trunk of a peculiar kind of tree which is now no longer met with except in the Soudán. All this seems to indicate that the renovation of Egyptian society and the founding of Thebes constitute a political fact which points to an invasion from the south.

The history of Thebes may easily be traced on the monuments, temples and tombs which to this day overspread the site of that far-famed city. Nothing of greater antiquity is to be found at Thebes than the chambers cut in the rock and the funereal wells which served for the interment of the mummies of the XIth dynasty, and this part of the necropolis is already known to the reader under the name of Drah-abou'l-neggah. The XIIth dynasty is also represented here, though more important monumental traces of it are found at Karnak. Up to the invasion of the Shepherds (XVth dynasty), Thebes was able to hold her own, but at this point occurs a complete blank, and whether or not the savage invaders of Northern

Egypt ever came to Thebes, several centuries elapse during which the national spirit is extinguished. The legitimate kings who had probably taken refuge in regions still more remote than Thebes, and who could have retained but a feeble authority, were otherwise employed than in building temples or erecting palaces. Presently the XVIIIth dynasty becomes a second *renaissance* of Egyptian civilisation, and ushers in the era of the Amenophis' and the Thothmes'. Until this time, nothing seems to indicate that Thebes extended beyond the sanctuary of Karnak, and the tombs of the XIth dynasty do not convey the idea either of a large city or of a very advanced state of civilisation. But with the XVIIIth dynasty suddenly rises in its full extent and glory that city which will soon be unrivalled in Egypt. Amenophis I. constructed at Karnak a portion of the temple which is now destroyed, but the importance of which is borne witness to by the colossal proportions of that king's statue which adorns the south-west frontal of the third pylon to the south. Thothmes I. commenced, in front of the sanctuary of Karnak, that truly monumental series of halls, of pylons and of obelisks, which gives so imposing an appearance to that side of the edifice. Under the regency of the sister of the two succeeding Thothmes', the third pylon to the south and the lateral chambers of the sanctuary were commenced at Karnak. The singular temple of Deir-el-Bahari was founded to commemorate a successful expedition into the Pount country (Arabia Felix). But it was principally under Thothmes III. and Amenophis III. that the prosperity of Thebes increased. Thothmes III. enlarged Karnak and sketched out its general plan; and he also erected on the left bank a temple which no longer exists. He laid the foundations of the little temple of Medinet-Abou, and by his order several other temples were erected on those sacred sites to which the modern village of Karnak has given its name. Nor did Amenophis III. allow himself to be eclipsed by the glory of his ancestors. The whole of the southern portion of the temple of Luxor was built by him, and it is to him we owe the temple of Mout, the northern temple of Ammon and the Alley of Sphinxes which leads up to the temple of Khons at Karnak. The imposing edifice which stood behind the two celebrated colossi of the left bank, was also built by Amenophis III. There are no records of the schism of Amenophis IV. at Thebes, beyond the traces of that puerile fanaticism which everywhere effaced the name of Ammon; but under Horus, who re-established the ancient religion upon its former footing, the luxurious capital received fresh embellishments. At Karnak, the two southern pylons and the avenue of Sphinxes, which connects the first pylon with the temple of Mout, were constructed. Nor was a similar spirit wanting under the XIXth dynasty. Rameses I. inaugurated the series of royal tombs in the principal valley of Bab-el-Molouk. He erected at Karnak the pylon which precedes the hypostyl hall, and it is most probably to him that we owe the conception of the really gigantic plan of this hall. Under Sethi I. the art of the sculptor and of the engraver maintained on the walls of the monuments of Thebes that perfection which we have already remarked at Abydos. It was also Sethi I. who commenced the construction of the hall of columns at Karnak; he erected seventy-eight out of the one hundred and thirty-four columns which make this hall the master-piece of Egyptian architecture. It was also Sethi I. who raised the temple of Goornah to the memory of his father, Rameses I. At Bab-el-Molouk he excavated in the rock itself that celebrated tomb which is at once the delight of the Egyptologist on account of the abundance of the inscriptions it contains, and his despair because of the mutilations to which it is daily subjected at the hands of travellers. Rameses II. was too much occupied in the provinces of Egypt, where his name is met with at almost every step, to have left at Thebes any trace worthy of the renown of him who was the Sesostris of the Greeks. He, however, completed the hypostyl hall of Karnak and built the surrounding wall of the temple; he also constructed a portion of Luxor. The decoration of his tomb, grand as the general plan may be, is mean and poorly conceived; but this inferiority is compensated by the Rameseum which does full justice to the reputation of the glorious son of Sethi I. The successors of Rameses II. added nothing of any importance to the existing monuments of Thebes, and it was not until Rameses III. appeared that the temple of Khons and the temple of the principal court of Karnak were founded. Then it was that Medinet-Abou was built, and then also was excavated at Bab-el-Molouk that celebrated tomb which is now known by the name of Bruce's, or the Harpist's tomb.

Here ends the period of Thebes' greatest magnificence and splendour. True, under the XXIInd dynasty, the Bubastites will construct the large court which precedes the temple of Karnak, and in due time Tahraka will engrave his cartouches on the same temple, as also at Medinet-Abou. And later on, the Saïtes of the XXVIth dynasty will raise here and there some sanctuaries now almost in ruins; and lastly the Ptolemies will mark their passage by the erection of the temple of Deir-el-Medineh and the two handsome portals which so magnificently usher in Karnak. But for all that, the grandeur of Thebes is already a thing of the past. At the death of Assarhaddon, Sardanapalus seizes on the city which he sacks, and which is subsequently restored by Tahraka, only to be retaken by the Ninevite conqueror. No real proof exists of the devastation which a somewhat exaggerated tradition assigns to Cambyses; it is possible, however, that this conqueror violated some of the tombs of Bab-el-Molouk, and that the Theban necropolis in particular suffered from his ravages. The siege and sack of Thebes by Ptolemy Lathyrus was the last and most supreme act of violence inflicted on the city of the Thothmes' and the Amenophis'. After that time Thebes had no place in history. Its downfall, which commenced with the high priests of the XXth dynasty, was complete before the commencement of the Christian era; for Strabo found nothing remaining of Thebes but a collection of villages disseminated over its ruins.

In its character of a sacerdotal city Thebes was called in Egyptian ▢ *Pir Amen* (the abode of Ammon), ▢ *No Amen* (the city of Ammon, Διόσπολις); but in its character of the capital of an administrative province it was called ▢ a word which should be transcribed *T"am* according to Mr. Birch, *Uas* according to M. Brugsch, and *Obé* according to M. Chabas. One of its quarters, that which spreads itself over the right bank of the river, received the name of *Apetu*, a name rendered most familiar to us by the legends which cover the monuments of Thebes.

The name given to Thebes in the Bible is

No-Amen, or simply *No*. The second of these names originates in the popular name of *No*, that is to say *the city par excellence*, which we find employed in the hieroglyphs, to designate Thebes, especially in the life-time of those sacred writers who make use of the name. A far more difficult matter it is to determine to what Egyptian prototype the name of Θήβη, Θῆβαι refers, so well known among the Greeks. It was certainly through Homer that this name became current in the Hellenic world, and took root there. But from what source did Homer borrow it in the first instance? M. Chabas derives it from the *Obé* already mentioned, placing the feminine article T before it. But could the name of a province be thus applied to a town? In Tahraka's time, Thebes was called by its popular name of *No*, but previously, and after the time of Amenophis III., the monuments designate it as *Tema*, another way of expressing the city *par excellence*. Was it then in *Tema* that Homer found that name which to his Grecian ears would sound very much like the Θῆβαι of Bœotia? One would fain believe it. The permutation of the M and of the B is one of the most frequently occurring philological facts. Was not the personage, who in the Hebrew text of the Bible is called Nemrod, designated in the Septuagint Νεβρώδ? Have we not both χνούβις and χνούμις? Is not *Berua* the native name of Meroë? Examples of this kind might be multiplied *ad infinitum*. The Egyptian *Tema* might thus have become *Teba*, and Homer, perhaps almost unconsciously, may have given to the capital of Egypt the name which in its signification of *the city* corresponds exactly with that of Medyneh, by which the Arabs of our time designate Cairo.

The position which the principal divinity of Thebes occupies in the Egyptian pantheism is well defined. Ammon is the visible, and so to speak, the tangible form of the creative force in nature. In him is symbolised that hidden spring which presses all things forward towards light and life. He is therefore perfectly typified by the sun. Mout and Khons are associated with him in his character as an eternal god. Mout is the mother; she is the recipient in which is accomplished the mystery of creation. Khons is Ammon himself as the offspring of the other two divine personages. Being at once his own father and his own son, this god of Thebes has neither beginning nor end, that is to say he is uncreate and eternal.

On arriving at Thebes, the right bank of the river and the left bank are successively visited, and Luxor being situated at the exact place where boats generally stop, naturally receives the traveller's first visit.

LUXOR.—Overwhelmed by the mass of modern erections which have invaded it like a rising tide, the temple of Luxor offers but a slight interest to the visitor. Its plan is very irregular, owing it is supposed to the fact that it was originally built at the edge of the river, and rising abruptly from a quay, was made to follow its windings.

The temple of Luxor was founded by Amenophis III., who constructed the whole of the southern part, including the heavy colonnade which overlooks the river. To Rameses II. we are indebted for the remaining portion, namely, the two obelisks, the pylon, the colossi and the large court which the mosque by which it has been invaded so unfortunately conceals. It is true, the cartouches of Alexander II. are found on the walls of the sanctuary, and those of

Amentouankh occur also in other parts of the
building, together with those of his brother
Horus, of Sabacon the Ethiopian, and of Psammetichus I. But none of these kings added in
any way to the construction of Luxor; they
simply made use of such portions of the wall as
had been left blank by their predecessors, by
engraving their name there; or they restored
some portion of the temple which was falling
into decay.

Let us add here that Luxor, as is very well
known, is the centre of a more or less legitimate
traffic in antiquities. Excavations being absolutely forbidden throughout Egypt, there is no
doubt that Luxor possesses certain manufactures
where statuettes, stelæ and scarabœi are imitated
with a dexterity which often deceives even the
most experienced antiquarian.

KARNAK.—The afternoon may be spent at
Karnak. Karnak is the most wonderful pile of
ruins which can be imagined, and it is even
chiefly on this account that it should be visited.
For it is simply impossible to attempt to unravel
at Karnak, as we have done at Denderah, a plan,
a unity, or a fixed design. The unity, if it ever
existed, is now entirely lost, not only on account

of the devastation which the temple has undergone, but because of the many successive epochs which have overlaid each other during its existence. The professed antiquarian therefore will alone be able to gather something from Karnak, but the ordinary traveller must be content to gaze at this temple as a monument of unparalleled grandeur, whose vast proportions and bewildering mass of ruins quite overpower the imagination. In fact, one has never seen enough of Karnak, and the more often one visits it the more stupendous it appears.

We cannot leave a building of this importance without lingering over some of its details. We will therefore briefly point out the route the traveller should take from Luxor, and the principal objects which he will pass on the way, more particularly deserving of his attention.

The best route to follow lies along the path that leads from Luxor to the modern village of Karnak, passing along the avenue of ram-headed sphinxes which date from the reign of Amenophis III., until he reaches the foot of the handsome portal or gateway which divides this avenue from the temple of Khons. After visiting this temple the traveller should proceed towards the north by the side of some modern hovels built over the ruins of the ancient city. He will thus penetrate into the great temple by its principal entrance, which is the western portal. The study of the grand temple being the chief object of the excursion, the traveller should leave no spot of this celebrated monument unvisited, and quitting the temple by an opening in the northern side of the surrounding wall, should devote a few minutes to the ruins of the temple of Ammon, and the monumental portal which forms the extreme boundary of the temple on this side; then returning towards the south, and bearing slightly to the left, still keeping outside the temple, he will follow along the ruins of the encircling wall to the east, until he reaches the small lake; he will then visit the third pylon, so remarkable for its colossal statues, and crossing the avenue of human-headed sphinxes which belong to the reign of Horus, he will finish his exploration by visiting the temple of Mout.*

The points which the traveller will find most

* Under the title of *A Topographical Survey of Karnak* I have published a detailed map of this temple with an explanatory text, minutely describing a systematic visit to the temple, of which I am only able here to give a brief outline.

interesting and worthy of study in the route just traced out are as follows :—

I. Temple of Khons.—This temple was constructed by Rameses II., by whom also it was founded, and we have every reason to believe that before his death the entire work was finished, including the pylon itself. The decoration of the temple of Khons furnishes us with the most useful information concerning the great historical fact which pervades the annals of the XXth dynasty in its latter period—we allude to the decline of the royal power under the Rameses', and the ever-increasing usurpation of authority by the priests of Ammon. At the end of the temple, that is to say, near the hall of eight columns, the decorations present no special interest. Rameses III., Rameses IV., Rameses XIII. are there represented in adoration before the local divinity. But a closer study of this hall gives rise to a suspicion that we have before us a series of facts as yet without precedent in Egyptian history. For the first time, a high-priest, Her-Hor, actually occupies the place on the walls of the temple invariably reserved for the sovereign. True, in the hall of the eight columns, the high priest has not yet appropriated to himself any of the royal titles, and it is together in his own name and in that of the reigning king that he addresses his speech to the god. But in the first hall, the one immediately following the pylon, the usurpation becomes flagrant. Here all disguise is thrown aside, and Her-Hor appears with the uræus or sacred asp on his brow, and his name enclosed within the double cartouche. The high priest Pinet'hem, who was soon to become king, is depicted on the pylon.

II. THE GREAT TEMPLE.—In its entire length, and including the dependencies to the east and to the west, the temple of Karnak cannot measure less than 608 mètres, or 1995 English feet. It measures 366 mètres by 106, or upwards of 1200 feet by 348 in that portion which is enclosed by the surrounding wall of stone, and this constitutes the true dimensions of the edifice.

The great temple should be entered by the western portal which we know already as the principal pylon. The ruins of the temple will then develop themselves before the visitor in the order which we shall endeavour to indicate, taking as our guide the subjoined plan.

The Pylon and the large Court.—These are marked A and B in our plan. Until the XXIInd dynasty the grand temple of Karnak had no other frontage than the pylon C, which dates from the time of Rameses I., and the remains of which may be seen at the bottom of the court. In front of this stood, apparently unconnected with the main building and as if dropped down there by chance, the temple D, to the left on entering the court, which dates from the reign of Sethi II. (XIXth dynasty) and the temple E to the right, which was founded by Rameses III. (XXth dynasty). To the Bubastites (XXIInd dynasty) is due the honour of having constructed the two fine enclosing walls to the north and to the south. Tahraka erected the double colonnade in the centre of the court, and the Ptolemies commenced the construction of that immense pylon to the west, which has remained unfinished.

The Hypostyl Hall (F).—This is the most spacious hall that the Egyptians ever constructed. It measures 102 mètres by 51, or 334 English feet by 167. The most ancient cartouches found here are those of Sethi I. (XIXth dynasty). Certain indications would lead one to believe that Sethi was only the constructor of this hall, and that to Rameses I. belongs the glory of having conceived the plan. Originally, the hall was entirely covered in, and daylight only entered by the grated windows, some remaining portions of which may still be seen on one side of the central nave. An obscure light, somewhat less dim than at Denderah, must have been all that was permitted to penetrate into the hall, thus adding to the general effect by softening the vivid colouring of the paintings with which the columns and ceilings are adorned.

Two large portals opened out from the centre of the side walls to the south and north of the Hall of Columns. Passing through these, the visitor will be enabled to study successively the bas-reliefs of the external wall to the south, as well as those of the external wall to the north.

The Bas-reliefs of the external southern wall of the Hypostyl Hall (J).—On the western side of this wall near the door opening out of the large court will be found a picture worthy of the visitor's attention. This picture was sculptured in remembrance of a victorious campaign against Palestine made by the first king of the XXIInd dynasty (called in the Bible Shishak). On the right, Shishak himself is represented raising his arm to strike a group of prisoners who are kneeling at his feet. On the left, Ammon of Thebes, and the Thebaid personified by a female figure holding in her hand the quiver, the bow, and the battle-axe, present themselves before him. Nearly 150 personages, whose heads only are visible, and whose bodies are, as it were, hidden behind a sort of castellated oval, representing a fortress or town, follow these two divinities. The inscriptions explain the scene. The gods themselves it is who bring to Shishak the towns which he has taken in his campaign. So many castellated cartouches, so many localities conquered. This picture possesses a peculiar interest of its own which must not be passed over in silence. In the 29th cartouche Champollion had read *Joudah-Melek*, and he concluded that the head which surmounted this cartouche was the portrait of the king of Judah himself, conquered by Shishak. But the researches of M. Brugsch have shown that *Joudah--Melek* is, like all the other names, without exception, the name of a locality in Palestine, and that there is nothing to justify the idea that in the personage who serves to symbolise this locality we have a portrait of Jeroboam. We may add that the sculptor has given a very similar expression to all the 150 heads, reminding one of the general type of the vanquished people, but a correct idea of the true physiognomy of these nations may be gathered from the study of the heads of those personages, evidently more carefully drawn, over whom the triumphant Pharaoh is raising his battle-axe.

The same wall is prolonged towards the east and is soon met by another wall which cuts it at right angles. Mounting on this latter wall, and looking towards the north, the visitor will have on his right a long text (H) which is nothing less than a copy of the famous poem of *Pen-ta--our*, a literary work composed by a poet of that name in honour of a feat of arms accomplished by Rameses II. in the fifth year of his reign, during his campaign against the Khetas. To the left (G) will be found what remains of the bas-reliefs representing episodes of another campaign, bearing no date, against the same people. At our feet lies the stela where is engraved with all the monumental solemnity of the time the treaty of peace concluded between Rameses II. and Kheta-sar, king of the

Khetas, in the 21st year of the reign of the Egyptian monarch.

The Bas-reliefs of the external wall to the north of the Hypostyl Hall (K). — These bas-reliefs contain the most precious records we possess of the reign of Sethi I. Here are represented, without any strict regard for their chronological or topographical order, Sethi's campaigns in Western Asia against the *Remenen* (the Armenians), the *Schasou* (the Arabs of the desert), the *Ruten* (the Assyrians), the *Khetas* (the Hittites of the Bible). This precious series of pictures is unfortunately much mutilated. Some among them, however, may still be made out which are deserving of the visitor's attention. The scene is laid in the country of the Remenen, Sethi having carried his victorious arms into that region. The first picture shows us the Remenen cutting down the trees of their forests, which they are bound to deliver to the conqueror, probably for the building of his houses. Sethi is on his chariot, his horses (the first of which is called the *Strength of Thebaïd*) bears him into the thickest of the fray. The foes are the Schasou. Sethi pursues them and pierces them with his arrows.

Those who escape precipitate themselves into the fortress of Kanana where they take refuge. Next comes another battle scene. The enemies are the people of the Kharo country. They fall pierced with the darts of the king. The Kharo country becomes henceforth a province of the Egyptian empire, and the fortresses taken by Sethi exchange their names for others made out of that of the victorious Pharaoh. Another campaign, this time against the *Ruten* (Assyrians) " who had not known Egypt." The prisoners are led forward in chains to be presented to the deities of Thebes. The victorious king returns to Egypt; he stops at *Ouat'i-en--Sethi*, and passes by another fortress called *Ta-sam-ef-en-pa* ... and a third called *Pa-ma*, until he at last reaches a walled-in town of which the name is partly lost (*Pithom-n...*) preceded by numerous prisoners from all nations. Here, near a stream of water swarming with crocodiles, he receives the principal functionaries of Egypt who have come to welcome him. A grand symbolic scene is here enacted; the king raises his battle-axe over a group of prisoners whom he has seized by the hair of their heads, and whom he is about to offer in sacrifice to the god of Thebes. More war scenes follow; the king is seen doing battle with enemies mounted on chariots, &c., &c.

The Passage between the two Pylons (L).—It is bounded on each side by a pylon; in the centre rose two obelisks, one of which is now overthrown. A huge block of granite in its original place in front of the obelisk which is still standing leads one to imagine that a colossal statue was formerly erected here, like the one at Luxor.

The first pylon (M) dates from the reign of Amenophis III., and before the grand hall was constructed it served as the façade of the temple itself. The chronological order of the pylons is thus rigorously observed. The first pylon which presents itself when one enters the temple is of the time of the Lagides (or Ptolemies), the second dates from Rameses I. and the third from Amenophis III. Unfortunately, nothing now is left but ruins, and all that we can gather from the remains of some inscriptions sculptured on the south-east façade of the pylon is that Amenophis III. had reserved this side of the monument which he was building, in order to engrave there the list of donations made by him to the temple of Ammon at Thebes. The king enumerates a vast quantity of rare stones and precious metals, which served to embellish the sacred edifice. Their number was indeed considerable; for example, mention is made of 4820 *uten* of turquoise, 3623 *uten* of a stone called *henti*. These donations were made after the campaign against the Asiatics, the booty of which served to enrich the temple of Karnak.

The second pylon (N) is in such a state of ruin that its plan is hardly discernible; it dates from the time of Thothmes I.; the portal which stands before it was constructed by Thothmes IV., and was altered under the XXVth dynasty by Sabacon.

Of the two obelisks attached to the pylon of Thothmes I., one only remains standing, its four sides being decorated with three columns of hieroglyphs. The central column contains nothing but the names and titles of the royal founder of the pylon, while those on each side show us some rather confused cartouches, among which the names of Rameses VI. may be noticed somewhat indistinctly engraved over those of Rameses IV. Upon the many fragments of the fallen obelisk which strew the ground may still be read the legends of Thothmes III.

The Hall of Caryatides. (O).—This might equally well be called the *Hall of the Obelisks*, or *of the Fourteen Columns*. The construction of this part of the temple belongs to Thothmes I. The two pylons by which it was shut in to the east and to the west were standing, as well as the fourteen columns, when the celebrated regent, the daughter of this same Thothmes, and sister of the two succeeding princes of that name, raised in the centre of this Hall the two most gigantic obelisks which exist. One of them has fallen down, and travellers scarcely notice it; the other, which is still standing, is known as the obelisk of *Hatasou*.

The obelisk of Heliopolis is 66 ft. 6 inches in height, the obelisk of Luxor in Paris is 75 feet, that of St. Peter's in Rome 82 feet 9 inches, and that of St. Jean de Lateran in Rome 105 feet 6 inches, but the obelisk of Hatasou is 108 feet 10 inches, and is therefore the highest obelisk known. The precision with which it is put on its base is remarkable; it is in the very axis of the temple, and this precision, considering the really enormous weight of the monolith, affords evidence of the use of mechanical appliances most exact as well as most powerful. The legends which cover it from top to bottom consist only of dedicatory formulas in the name of Hatasou (XVIIIth dynasty, about the year 1660 B.C.), the regent whose name deservedly ranks with those of Thothmes and Amenophis. Round the lowest part of the obelisk runs an inscription in horizontal lines covering the whole of its four sides. This inscription makes us acquainted with certain facts which should not be passed over, and which may be interpreted thus :—1°. The summit of the obelisk was covered over with "pure gold taken from the chiefs of the nation." Unless this simply implies an apex overlaid with a casing of gilded copper, as the apex of the obelisk at Heliopolis must have been, this inscription possibly refers to the sphere (of gold?) which is represented on certain bas-reliefs at Sakkárah. 2°. The obelisk itself was no doubt gilded from top to bottom; in examining closely, one may notice that the hieroglyphs were carefully polished, and moreover that the plain surface of the monument was left comparatively rugged, from which it may be inferred that the plain surface, having a coating of white stucco the like of which may be seen on so many Egyptian monuments, alone received this costly embellishment of gilding, the hieroglyphs themselves retaining the original colour and actual surface of the granite. 3°. The inscription further states, as a fact worthy of being transmitted to posterity, the incredibly short space of time in which both obelisks, the one we have described and the other which matched it, were actually completed and erected, viz., "in seven months, from the very beginning, when first extracted from the quarry in the mountain." It is perhaps superfluous to add that the caryatides, some of which still remain, are nothing but representations of Thothmes I. in the character of Osiris as king of all ages and arbiter of man's destiny.

Hall of the Eighteen Columns (P).—This portion of the temple has greatly suffered and does not present any particular interest. This Hall was founded by Thothmes I., whose cartouches are still to be seen on the two polygonal columns sunk in the masonry to the right and to the left of the entrance. The work was completed by his son, the same who rendered the name of Thothmes so famous.

The granite Chambers and their Dependencies.— We here enter a part of the temple of which the

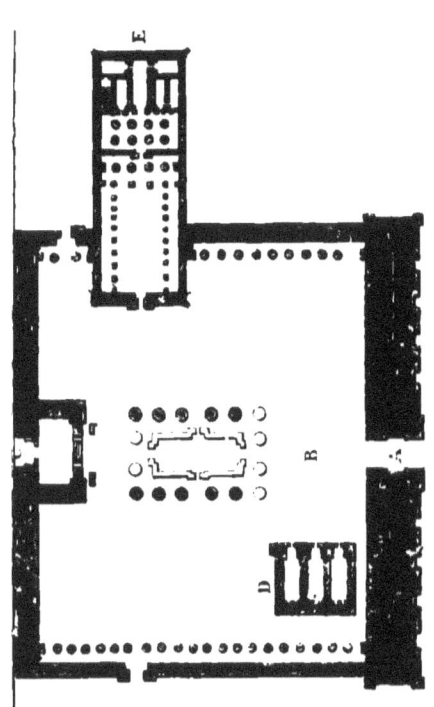

little hall R is evidently the nucleus and the centre. This hall was constructed by Thothmes III., and if no other cartouches but those of Philip Aridœus are now to be read here, it is owing to the circumstance that the walls of the chamber having been found in an unsafe condition were reconstructed by this brother of Alexander.

Access is obtained to that part of the temple which contains the hall R through a pylon (Q). This pylon is the last of the series of monumental portals which lead from the exterior of the temple up to the sanctuary. This one is smaller than its neighbour which in its turn is not so high as the pylon which precedes it. Thus from the entrance to the end of the temple the pylons decrease in height progressively and symmetrically. The first is the truly gigantic pylon which forms the western limit of the temple. The last is the somewhat mean construction which now stands before us.

The western frontage of the pylon Q is covered with representations before which it is impossible not to stop. On one side are represented 115 personages tied together by their arms and by their necks. The opposite side is covered in like manner with 115 other personages. They all bear, attached to their breast, an embattled scutcheon in which some hieroglyphs are inscribed. There can be no doubt as to the meaning of these inscriptions. The 115 personages to the right symbolise an equal number of towns taken by Thothmes III. during his campaign in the south of Egypt; the 115 to the left personify so many localities conquered by the same prince during one of his campaigns in the north.

The list of the countries to the south may be divided into three parts. The first comprises *Kousch the bad*, and does not carry us beyond the limits of modern Tigrè; forty-six names are given, among them Adulis (n° 2). The second part embraces the Pount country which M. Brugsch identifies as Arabia Felix, or the Yemen; we have here forty geographical names. The third part takes us into Libya. Libya, according to Herodotus, was inhabited by two indigenous races—to the south the Ethiopians; to the north the Libyans. It is doubtless to the Ethiopian region of Libya that the third part of the list of Karnak refers.

The list of the northern countries will be found still more interesting. The horizontal line of hieroglyphs which runs along the upper part forms the general title which may be thus translated: "List of the countries of the Upper Ruten which his Majesty (Thothmes III.) confined within the town of Megiddo the wretched, and whose children have been carried away as living captives by his majesty to the fortress of *Souhen* at Thebes, at the time of his first victorious expedition, in accordance with the order of his father Ammon who guided him in the right way." There can be no misgiving as to the exact period of the events in memory of which this list was drawn up. These events date from the reign of Thothmes III., and refer to the first out of the thirteen or fourteen campaigns of that prince. Nor need we hesitate as to the name of the country which is here designated, it being the same which the legends call High Ruten, or Upper Ruten; and the country corresponding to that which the Egyptian texts call Upper Ruten can be identified at a glance. We have before us, most accurately rendered by the hieroglyphic names: Kadesch (n° 1), Megiddo (2), Beth-Tapuah (6), Juta (9), Damascus (13), Beyrout (19), Ashtaroth-Karnaïm (27), Hatzor (32), Kennereth, (34), Schunem

(38), Nain (45), Acco (Acre, 46), Jaffa (62), Lod (64), Ono (65), Socho (67), Henganim (70), Migdal (71), Guerar (80), Rehoboth (87), Beth-Markaboth (94), Beth-Hanath (109), Ziph (114). Beyrout lies quite to the north, Rehoboth is as far to the south. To the west we are carried to the shores of the Mediterranean and to the east we only just cross the Jordan. No doubt whatever can exist. If these limits are not precisely the same as the Xth chapter of Genesis assigns to the land of Canaan, at all events these 115 names carry us to the very centre and heart of that far famed country. The data are certainly very precise with regard both to chronology and geography. In fact, this list of 115 names is nothing less than a synoptical table of the Promised Land, made 270 years before the Exodus.

When the pylon is passed, on turning sharply to the left, the last lines of a very long inscription will be found which commences at the further extremity of the wall. In spite of many mutilations, too often intentional, which this inscription has undergone, it is still one of the most valuable among the many texts with which the walls of the temple of Karnak abound. We find here inscribed a succinct account of all the wars undertaken by Thothmes III. from the twenty-second to the fortieth year of his reign. Fourteen campaigns are enumerated. As the inscription is above all due to the anxiety of Thothmes to apprise posterity of the numberless gifts with which he enriched the treasure of Ammon, the author of the text enumerates with minute care the booty taken from the enemy, and the tribute imposed upon him. He gives the number of prisoners made, the horses, the cattle, the ivory, the ebony, the precious woods, the rare stones, the chariots, the weapons, the furniture, the utensils, the corn, wine, honey, and odoriferous perfumes sent into Thebes. Although, in the account given by Tacitus, the name of Rameses is quoted, and not that of Thothmes, there is no doubt that it was the Karnak text that the priests showed to Germanicus. " *Legebantur*," says Tacitus, " *et indicta gentibus tributa, pondus argenti et auri, numerus armorum equorumque, et dona templis, ebur atque odores, quasque copias frumenti et omnium utensilium quæque natio penderet.*"

The large Court to the East.—It is a mistake to consider the granite chamber already mentioned (R) as the actual sanctuary of the great temple of Karnak. The sanctuary of the grand temple was anterior to Philip, anterior even to Thothmes; it ranked among the oldest edifices in Egypt. since it dated from the second king of the XIIth dynasty. It was built of sandstone, and stood in the centre of the large court to the east (S). Its renown, its antiquity, and probably also its riches had the effect of attracting, more than any other part of the temple. the attention of every conqueror who invaded Thebes, and it has disappeared to its very foundations. With the exception of two or three shafts of shattered columns, on which may still be traced the legend of Usertasen I., nothing remains to recall its memory.

The Eastern Gallery and its Dependencies (T). —All those passages, chambers, and galleries which form the extreme eastern boundary of the grand temple of Karnak were set apart for religious purposes. The processions must have passed through the galleries, while some of the chambers served either for the manipulation and preparation of the offerings, or as a depository for the sacred objects which were used at the celebration of the fêtes. This part of the temple was the work of Thothmes III., some few points of which are especially deserving of the traveller's attention, such as :—

The Chamber X., the sub-basement of which is remarkable. Thothmes depicted here the fauna and flora of Upper Ruten, as also of an unknown country called *To-Nuter* (the divine land), a country which must be sought for either in the southern extremity of the Arabian peninsula, or on the borders of the Persian gulf. These curious representations are not to be met with in any other temple of Egypt. The two fine sphinxes in pink granite which now adorn the principal court of the Boolák Museum were found standing between the columns of this chamber.

The Chamber U.—All the pictures bear the name of Alexander II., but the inscriptions tell us that the chamber was falling into ruins when that prince caused it to be reconstructed.

The Chamber V.—A smaller chamber was enclosed in chamber V. Some thirty years ago it was taken down and transported to Paris, and is known in scientific circles as the *Hall of Ancestors*. Thothmes is there represented as offering homage to sixty kings chosen from among his predecessors on the throne.

We will conclude this notice of the grand temple of Karnak with one more observation. Every one is awe-struck at the marvellous heap of stones which makes this grand temple at Karnak, from a certain point of view, the most picturesque monument of Egypt. Is this stupendous ruin the result of an earthquake? Was the destruction of Karnak brought about by the ravages of Ptolemy Lathyrus, and the pitiless sack to which that king delivered the city of Thebes, after a siege of seven months? Was it not rather owing to the faulty construction of the temple, and to its position with regard to the Nile?* This last hypothesis is the most probable; for the Pharaonic temples were, generally speaking, built with extreme carelessness. The western pylon, for instance, has given way, simply on account of the hollowness of its construction, and the inward inclination of the walls, far from supplying an element of strength, proved rather a source of insecurity. For many years the grand temple of Karnak has, more than any other Egyptian temple, been assailed by the infiltration of the Nile, whose water, saturated as it is with nitre, eats away the sandstone. The temple of Karnak, therefore, has suffered in an exceptional degree from the effects

* The pavement of the temple is about six feet below the present level of the surrounding plain.

of time through the negligence of its constructors, and above all through its relative position towards the Nile; and as the same causes produce incessantly the same effects, one may predict that a time will come when, one catastrophe following another, the magnificent hypostyl hall, whose columns are already so much eaten away at their base, will give way and collapse altogether, as has been the case with the columns of the grand western court.

III. The Ruins to the North.—Our route now lies to the north of the great temple and in the very midst of the ruins with which this portion of Karnak is strewn. The two sanctuaries which lie to the left are of the XXVIth dynasty, and possess but little interest. The temple which abuts upon the encircling wall was begun by Thothmes III., and successively enlarged by Sabacon and the Ptolemies. On the other side of the same encircling wall, and corresponding with six doorways pierced in it, are six small temples all in ruins, which belong to the period comprised between the XXIInd and XXVIth dynasties. Again, quite to the north stands an edifice dedicated, like the grand temple of Karnak, to the principal personage of the Theban triad. This edifice was founded, and probably entirely constructed by Amenophis III. Under the Ptolemies, the front part of the monument, including the chamber which is surrounded with columns, was repaired in conformity with the style of the period, as was also, in the same manner and at the same time, the monumental portal to the extreme north. Already, in front of the temple properly so called, Rameses II. had raised the two granite obelisks, of which nothing but the *débris* is now to be seen. The temple itself is in a state of utter ruin; in certain parts the walls have disappeared to their very foundations, in others they have preserved only a foot or two of their original height. However, one entire gateway may still be seen standing, as well as a few remains of rather high walls at the south west corner.

IV. THE RUINS TO THE SOUTH.—We now retrace our steps southwards, that is to say towards Luxor whence we started, and continuing along the wall which bounds the grand temple to the east, we find our way to the three remaining points which we have yet to visit: the lake, the four pylons to the south, and the temple of Mout.

The Lake.—The sacred barks of the temple

went in procession on the lake during the fête days. This lake had been dug out by Thothmes III., who, in one of the inscriptions of the temple, boasts of having himself presided over the commencement of the works. There is no canal connecting this lake with the Nile, its waters maintaining their level by gradual infiltration alone.

The Four Pylons to the South.—These are all more or less in ruins. Judging by the position they occupy in the general plan of Karnak, they were evidently intended as a link between the temple of Mout and the grand temple; but the singular divergence of their axis constitutes a problem not so easily solved. Perhaps, on the vast space of ground left bare by the side of the grand temple, these pylons were erected as so many triumphal arches, intended to perpetuate the glory of their royal founders. This seems more than probable, especially if one tries to recall in imagination the two high towers of the pylon, their large central entrance gate, and the heroic battle scenes with which their sides were covered. The two southernmost pylons date from the reign of Horus (XVIIIth dynasty). The third was begun by Queen Hatasou, after she had been associated on the throne with her father Thothmes I. The fourth is of the time of Thothmes III. Numberless inscriptions, overlaying each other in the names of Sethi I., Rameses II., Rameses IV. and Rameses VI., are to be seen at various points, particularly on the second of these pylons.

Colossal statues adorned each side of the four pylons. These are destroyed, or, at least, any portion that remains is in a deplorable state of mutilation. The two statues of fine white limestone, which are attached to the northern side of the first pylon, represent Rameses II. Six colossi once stood in front of the southern side of the third pylon, but those to the west have alone left any visible remains. The first represents Thothmes II. seated. The second is the colossus of Amenophis I., of which we have already spoken; and on the base of the third may be read the cartouches of Thothmes III.

Between the first and second pylons, in the centre of the enclosing wall that connects them, is a temple of peculiar construction, of which it may be interesting to point out the special purpose. The whole of this temple belongs to the time of Amenophis II.; in it we may recognise a perfect model of that sort of resting place where, during the grand commemorative fêtes of the principal temple, the processions halted for the performance of some special ceremonial.

The Temple of Mout.—We have now reached the southernmost extremity of Karnak. The temple of Mout has suffered more than any of those previously described, and we cannot help feeling a still deeper regret at the ruined state to which it has been reduced when we reflect that here we have an entire temple, with its surrounding wall, its pylons, sphinxes and sanctuary, and even its lake. The temple of Ammon to the north of Karnak was founded by Amenophis III., and it is again the same king whose name we find given as the founder of the temple of Mout to the south.

The lion-headed figures which decorate the temple raise a problem which as yet has scarcely been solved. The first court was, so to speak, filled with these figures, as well as the second court and the two passages which run round the temple from east to west. They are all cut out of black granite, and are all almost exactly alike as to size and execution. Symmetrically arranged along the wall in a single, or sometimes in a double row, they sit so close together that their elbows almost touch. Finally, if we try to reconstruct the whole from the data furnished by such of the statues as still remain in their original position, and supply therefore reliable evidence, we shall find that the temple of Mout was originally adorned with no less than five hundred statues, uniformly representing a lion-headed goddess.

We now pass to the left bank of the river. Here the route varies with the season. When the Nile is low, and the western plain is dry, and especially when a landing can easily be effected on the left bank, immediately opposite Luxor, it is better to fix the head quarters at Luxor, as from that central spot the town itself can be visited as well as the left bank of the river. But when the Nile is overflowing its banks, and even for some time after its waters have begun to subside, the plain is covered with pools of water and traversed by numerous canals; nor is it an uncommon occurrence at that time of year for a boat starting from Luxor to run aground before reaching the opposite bank, and travellers have to be carried from the boats by the Arabs to a distance of perhaps two or three hundred yards. Therefore it is advisable when the Nile is full to leave Luxor and to seek a spot some three miles further down the stream, where a better landing may be effected, and whence easy access is obtained to the ruins. In other words, when the Nile is low the temples on the left bank may be visited from the south ; when the Nile is high it is as well, as we are about to do, to commence from the north.

The temples to be visited on the left bank are as follow :—

THE TEMPLE OF GOORNAH.—This is the most northerly of the temples on the left bank ; it is situated at the extremity of the cultivated land, and at the entrance of the gorge which leads to Bab-el-Molouk. Two pylons once stood in front of this temple, but a few stones are all that now remains to mark their place. Built at the same time as the temple of Sethi at Abydos, the temple of Goornah is likewise on a somewhat fantastical plan, the purport of which cannot be thoroughly realised, as the inscriptions in the interior throw no light on the details of those ceremonies for which either temple was set apart. This temple, like that of Abydos, is funereal in its character, and herein lies its originality ; for whilst at Abydos the deity of the temple is Osiris himself, king of the Egyptian infernal regions, here the deity of the temple is Rameses I. to whose memory the monument was raised by his son Sethi. The position of the temple on the borders of the desert and at the entrance to the necropolis is thus explained. The temple is, in fact, a cenotaph. We have had occasion more than once, in the early part of this work, to refer to that portion of the mastabah, so thoroughly distinct from the well, where on certain days in the year the relatives assembled and the defunct was treated almost as though he were still alive. The main idea of the temple of Goornah is in some respects the same, allowance being made for the interval which, from an Egyptian point of view, separates the king from his subjects. The temple of Goornah was, so to speak, haunted by the memory of Rameses I. It was the memory of this king that the faithful came to evoke on certain days prescribed by the rite. The mummy itself reposed afar off, deep down in the hypogeum of Bab-el-Molouk, just as in the mastabahs of the Ancient Empire the mummy reposed at the bottom of an inaccessible well.

The style of the bas-reliefs at Goornah also

recalls forcibly those at Abydos. On both sides one sees the same artistic design, the same largeness of treatment and the same delicacy of touch. After entering the hall of six columns by the central doorway, the visitor will find, on one of the walls of the third chamber to the right, an admirable head of Sethi, scarcely inferior to the most beautiful of those we have already admired on the walls of Abydos. Sethi, whose filial piety had raised this temple, left some portions unfinished; of these Rameses II. took possession, and, in his turn, dedicated them to the memory of his father Sethi.

THE RAMESEUM.—The Rameseum is reached from Goornah in following the edge of the cultivated land. The route lies past Drah-abou'l--Neggah, across a part of El-Assassif, and skirts the necropolis of Scheikh Abd-el-Goornah. Presently, some imposing ruins are reached, from the midst of which the colossal caryatides and the majestic columns stand out in golden relief against the neighbouring mountains—this is the Rameseum.

The Rameseum was erected by Rameses II., whose cartouches are sculptured on each of its walls; it was formerly styled the *Palace of*

Memnon, and the *Tomb of Osymandyas*, but it was much more appropriately called Rameseum by Champollion—a name it has retained.

The idea which presided at the construction of the temple of Goornah presided also at the erection of the Rameseum. Here also the temple is a cenotaph. Only, instead of being founded by the son of the deceased king, this temple is a monument raised by Rameses II. to himself. In speaking of the tombs of the Ancient Empire we stated that they were constructed by the defunct during his lifetime, a fact which is beyond dispute. When Ameni--Amenemha, for instance, relates at Beni-Hassan how, as general of infantry, he defeated the Ethiopians, and as moudir of the province of Sah he was generous to the widow and the orphan, it is not from the devotion of the survivors that this panegyric proceeds, it is Ameni-Amenemha himself who, in a sort of autobiography, thus extols his own virtues. In the same way, Rameses raises in the necropolis of Thebes, in the very centre of the district of the dead, a monument where after his death his subjects shall come and evoke his memory, and wherein he naturally displays his piety, his glory, and, as a matter of course, his campaigns. In fact, the Rameseum, whilst a funereal edifice in the main,· according to its founder's intention, becomes historical in its details, thanks to the numerous historical pictures which are sculptured on its walls.

Like the temple of Goornah, it was preceded by two pylons, now more or less demolished. The sculptures on the first of these pylons are only visible at a certain hour in the day when the light becomes sufficiently crisp. The sculptures are historical, and refer to one of the most remarkable episodes in the reign of Rameses II. The scene is laid in Syria, on the borders of a river which everything seems to point out as the Orontes. Rameses is present in person, and comes, fully armed, to dispute the possession of the country against a vast confederation of people designated under the generic name of Khetas. Kadesh is the nearest town. Through a concourse of circumstances which do not exactly reflect credit on the Egyptian generals, Rameses finds himself suddenly surrounded by his enemies. The soldiers who formed his escort had taken flight. Rameses stands alone, and "there is no one with him." With unreflecting valour he throws himself among the chariots. He kills the chiefs of "the vile Khetas," forces their troops to recross the river in hot haste, and by his personal courage turns the threatened rout into a complete victory. This brilliant feat of arms is what the first pylon of the Rameseum commemorates. On one side, Rameses is seen precipitating himself into the thickest of the fight; the enemy fly in terror; some are crushed under the feet of the horses, and under the chariot-wheels; others lie dead on the ground pierced with the arrows shot by the king's own hand; others again leap into the river and are drowned. On the opposite side, the king is represented seated on his throne; his officers come forward tendering their congratulations, but it is with reproofs that the king receives them: "Not one among you," he exclaims, "has behaved well in thus deserting me and leaving me alone in the midst of the enemy. The princes and captains did not join hands with me in fight; by myself have I done battle; I have put to flight thousands of nations, and I was all alone! . . ." In describing the temple of Luxor we have mentioned the two obelisks which stand before the pylon, and the pylon itself, but we omitted to add that the representations which cover the outer wall of this pylon are historical. It is to this same episode of the war with the Khetas that they refer, and Rameses is there also represented as accomplishing the exploit which he evidently considered one of the greatest events of his reign; for he reproduced it at the Rameseum, at Luxor, at Karnak, and at Ipsamboul, and we shall again find it recorded upon the second pylon of the temple we are now describing.*

What remains of the second pylon seems to preserve its equilibrium only by a miracle, and if we did not know that the artists who accompanied the French Expedition some seventy-five years ago saw it and sketched it in the same state in which we see it and sketch it at the present day, we should fear at every moment to see it fall. This second pylon gave access to a court surrounded by pilasters supporting large figures of Rameses invested with the attributes of Osiris—an arrangement in harmony with the funereal character of the temple.

In front of the pylon, that is to say on the

* This episode is the subject of the poem of *Pen-ta-our*, of which we have spoken above (page 165).

eastern side, stood the most gigantic statue that the Egyptians ever carved out of a single block of granite. It measured 17 met. 53 cent., or 57 feet 5 inches in height, and its weight could not be less than 1,217,872 kilos, or upwards of 1,198 tons. Rameses, it need hardly be said, is the personage represented. Unfortunately, of one of the most prodigious works which have come from the Egyptian chisel nothing now remains but fragments. The face even is mutilated, and in looking at this enormous monolith broken in pieces, the victim of an implacable fury, one does not know which to wonder at most, the patience and strength of those who brought it entire from A souân to serve as ornament to a temple, or the strength and patience of those who overthrew the monster and laid him low.

On the interior façade of the pylon, against which the colossus of Rameses rested, are sculptured numerous historical pictures, where we again find the episode of the battle against the Khetas. The light here is more favourable, and the details of the scene can be better studied. Rameses is in the centre of the affray, dealing death around him, and already numerous corpses strew the field of battle. Here Grabatousa, the armour-bearer of the prince of Kheta, falls pierced by the arrows of the king; there Rabsounma, captain of the archers, meets with the same fate. The Orontes lies in the path of the Khetas, who fly in disorder. They precipitate themselves into the stream, and on the other side of the river one sees being drawn out of the water one of the enemy's generals, whom his soldiers suspend with his head downwards, in order to expel the water which threatens to suffocate him. The episodes which the artist has introduced here and there with more industry than talent, are as numerous as they are interesting, witness the different portions of the large bas-reliefs which cover the pylon. In other parts of the edifice there are many religious scenes representing Rameses in adoration before the Theban gods, some lengthy lists of princes and princesses of the royal family, and an astronomical table which Biot's learned descriptions have rendered famous. The hall conducting to the ceremonial chambers of the temple has graceful columns with capitals of expanded flowers, which contrast favourably with the heavy columns of Karnak.

The Colossi.—The Colossi stood before the

pylon of a temple which has disappeared to the very foundations. It was built of limestone and owes its destruction to the value of its materials. The colossi are of breccia, a kind of puddingstone mixed with agate-like pebbles, and as they were of no use as food for the neighbouring limekilns, they have survived. Doubtless the temple, the entrance to which was so majestically guarded by these colossi, was to Amenophis III. what the Ramesseum was to Rameses II., and what Medinet-Abou was to Rameses III. It may therefore be inferred that the destruction of this edifice has deprived science of documents which would probably have thrown much light upon one of the most interesting reigns in Egyptian history.

Originally, the colossi were monoliths. The northern colossus having been robbed of its upper portion by an accident, to which we shall have occasion to refer presently, was restored with blocks of sandstone disposed in layers. Each colossus rests on a separate basis, also of breccia.

When these two statues stood in front of the pylon, rising so grandly from their base, they were 19 met. 60 cent. or 64 feet 4 inches high; that is to say, about the height of a five-storied house. Independently of their pedestal the statues themselves only measure 15 met. 60 cent., or 51 feet 2 inches. They are buried in the ground, like the temple of Karnak, to a depth of about 6 feet 3 inches. We need hardly add that both statues represent Amenophis III. seated in the hieratic posture. The figures at the side represent the mother and the wife of that sovereign.

The more northerly of the two statues is the *Colossus of Memnon*, so renowned among travellers who, in the two first centuries of the Roman dominion in Egypt, visited the land of the Pharaohs. Destined by Amenophis as an ornament to the façade of his temple, this colossus had remained known to all the world as the statue of Amenophis until the upper part was destroyed by an earthquake in the year 27 B.C.* Strange to say, this same accident by which the colossus was so materially damaged proved the chief cause of its celebrity. It soon became apparent that from the headless trunk a sonorous ringing sound, re-

* *Thebæ Ægypti usque ad solum dirutæ sunt*, says Eusebius. If the earthquake proved so violent, we may attribute to the same cause the fall of the pylon at Karnak, the accumulated stones of which impress one so strongly on entering the large court, although, as we have pointed out, Karnak has found its principal enemy in the nitre that corrodes the base of its walls.

sembling the human voice, was heard when the first rays of the morning sun fell upon the statue. Doubtless this sound was merely the result of the cracking of the stone, wet with the morning dew, under the influence of the rays of the sun. But by the Greeks and the Romans who visited Egypt at that time the phenomenon soon began to be looked upon in the light of a miracle. The colossus was situated in a district of Thebes called the *Memnonia*. Memnon was, according to the tradition accepted by foreigners, the legendary founder of the edifices of this part of the city. Was not the voice thus heard the plaintive voice of Memnon imploring his divine mother Aurora? The fame of the colossus soon spread abroad. From all parts of the known world people came to hear the marvellous voice, and the mania arose for engraving on the legs of the statue the tokens of admiration of those who were fortunate enough to become witnesses of this miracle. Eventually, after the lapse of two centuries, Septimius Severus, thinking to stay the plaintive cries of the hero, and to impart clearness and beauty to his voice, restored the colossus. He, however, only partially succeeded; the hero, it is true, no longer uttered his plaintive cries, but all sound was effectually smothered and for ever silenced under the blocks of sandstone which we see to this day.

One may easily see, on inspecting the legs of the colossus, how numerous were these tokens of admiration. Many of them are dated, the most ancient being of the time of Nero, the most recent of that of Septimius Severus. The reign of Hadrian alone added twenty-seven to the collection, and there are others, still more numerous, which are not accompanied by any date. Most frequently these inscriptions are in prose, and run thus : " Sabina Augusta, the consort of the Emperor Cæsar Augustus, has twice heard the voice of Memnon during the first hour." And again: "I, Vitalinus, epistrateges of Thebaid, with my wife, Publia Sosis, I have heard Memnon in the year III. . . . in the month of Pachon (or ninth month), twice at half past one o'clock." But sometimes also poetry is employed, and we may quote the two following samples: "I, Petronianus, who inherit from my father the name of Dillius, an Italian by birth, I honour thee with these elegiac verses, in offering to the god who speaks to me a poetical gift. But, in return, O king, grant me a long life! Many are they who come to this spot to know whether Memnon preserves a voice in that portion of his body which remains to him. As for him, seated on his throne, deprived of his head, he breaks into sighs to complain to his mother of the outrage of Cambyses, and when the brilliant sun shoots forth his rays, he announces the return of day to the mortals here assembled."—" Thy mother Aurora, the rosy-fingered goddess, O far-famed Memnon, has rendered thee vocal for me who was desirous to hear thee. In the twelfth year of the illustrious Antoninus, during the month of Pachon (the ninth month), reckoning thirteen days, twice, O divine being, have I heard thy voice when the sun left the majestic waves of the ocean. In olden times, Jupiter, the son of Saturn, made thee king of the East, and now thou art nothing but stone, and out of a stone proceeds thy voice. Gamella, in his turn, has written these verses, having come here with his beloved spouse Rafilla, and his children."

DEIR-EL-MEDINEH.—Between the colossi and Medinet-Abou, behind that part of the ancient necropolis called *Goornat-Mouraï*, is a small temple hidden in a hollow. It was begun by Ptolemy Philopater, and finished by his successors. The place which it occupies in the necropolis, and the presence of Osiris among the deities of the interior, undoubtedly mark this temple as a funereal monument. The inscriptions, however, give no certain clue to the definite intention nor to the general idea which it served to commemorate.

We would scarcely recommend it to the notice of the ordinary traveller, were it not that its elegant façade, constructed upon a design of which no better example can be found in Egypt, is well worth a visit. There is also a curious window, opening out of the southern wall of one of the inner chambers, which may be studied with advantage.

MEDINET-ABOU.—Proceeding from the north along the western side of Thebes, which is the route we are now following, one perceives from a distance, lying some way off to the south, a large sombre-coloured mound, out of which emerge here and there some constructions of a golden hue. This gloomy-looking mound is a Coptic village, which, at the downfall of the Egyptian religion, grew up all round and above a temple whose ruins we begin to discern, until it almost entirely buried it. The temple is that of Medinet-Abou, so called after the very village which, fungus-like, had fastened itself on to its ancient walls.

By many the temple of Medinet-Abou is considered a sort of Versailles, raised to celebrate the glory of Rameses III. But, in reality, Medinet--Abou is composed of two separate temples.

1°. *Temple of Thothmes III.*—The florid capitals of the columns standing at the end of the first court, as also the clumsy style of the sculptures and especially of the hieroglyphs, clearly indicate that the entrance is of the Roman period. In fact, the names of Titus, Hadrian, and Antoninus may be read in various parts of the court. A Roman origin also may be assigned to the half-finished pylon which succeeds the first court, although the portal placed between them dates on one side from the reign of Ptolemy Lathyrus, and on the other from that of Philip Auletes.

We next come upon a smaller court which terminates in a pylon of the most elegant construction. The dates here can only be arrived at, so to speak, by intuition. True, some few cartouches are visible here and there that belong to Tahraka (XXVth dynasty, 660 B.C.) and to Nectanebo II. (XXXth dynasty, 350 B.C.); but sometimes one has to discover the original owner of a cartouche which Ptolemy Lathyrus took from Nectanebo who himself had taken it from Tahraka.

Passing through the central doorway of the pylon across a third court, one enters the temple, properly so called. The most ancient cartouches found here are those of Thothmes II., whilst those of Thothmes III. are the most numerous. Then follow, down to Ptolemy Physcon, cartouches of almost every epoch, which are curiously entangled in the midst of the many restorations the temple has undergone. Having thus far ascertained the founder of the temple, and the different epochs with which it is associated, we may wonder for what purpose this little edifice was designed before Rameses III. erected so close to it the grand monument which now absorbs all the traveller's attention. The inscriptions throw no light on this point.

2°. *Temple of Rameses III.*—The temple of Rameses III. by its size, by the harmony of its parts, its historical importance, its style, and the variety of pictures with which it is adorned, is one of the monuments of Egypt that leave the most agreeable, and at the same time the most lasting impression on the traveller's mind. It consists of two parts separated by a court; the first, which is found immediately on entering the edifice by the main gateway, has been called the *Palace*. Next comes the real *Temple* ushered in by a magnificent pylon.

A. The Palace possesses all the characteristics of a regal habitation. Two large square towers, the four walls of which incline symmetrically towards a common centre, form the main body of the building. The architectural details are worthy of attention. Externally, especially on the north side, the windows are surrounded by singularly original and curious ornaments. On the upper stories are seen resting on the backs of recumbent prisoners slabs evidently intended to support the extremities of the verandah which must have extended over the entrance corridor, so as to shade the eastern façade from the sun. But it is chiefly in the interior chambers that the private character of the edifice is manifested. Here Rameses III. is really in his home surrounded by his family. One of his daughters brings him flowers; he plays draughts with another, and he is offered fruits by a third whom he caresses by way of thanks.

It is not to be expected that in a construction of such importance, Rameses should be unmindful of future history, or indifferent to the expediency of exhibiting himself as a conqueror. In fact, at the very entrance gate, Rameses is represented bringing to the gods the prisoners he has captured. With most remarkable skill the Egyptian sculptor has succeeded in giving to each one of these prisoners the distinctive type of his race. We must remember that we are here in the thirteenth century before our era, and the ethnologist will nowhere find more authentic specimens of the nations who then inhabited Western Asia, Libya, and the Soudân. At the most eastern entrance gate, the passage leading to the palace suddenly spreads itself out into two small square courts. The sculptures which adorn the western wall of these courts should be carefully studied; here especially will be found portraits of captives in true artistic style which must have been drawn from the life. To the right, that is to say on the northern side, are captives belonging to the nations of the Mediterranean, and to Western Asia; on the south side are those from Libya and the Kousch country. The former are thus described :—1°.

"The vile chief of the *Khetas*, a living prisoner;" he is full-faced and beardless; his ears are adorned with large rings, and his head is covered with a tight-fitting cap from which falls a tress of hair which hangs down his back. The Khetas formed a confederation of people who inhabited Syria and a part of Palestine.—2°. "The vile chief of the *Amaro* country" has a long face and pointed beard; this is the King of the Amorites, the inhabitants of the western shores of the Dead Sea.—3°. "The chief of the enemies from *T"akkara"* wears a quaintly-shaped cap, hollowed out at the side and flattened at the top; he has a round face and no beard. We are advancing towards the north, and the T'akkaraou represent the Teucrians who inhabited the coast of Asia Minor.—4°. "The country of the *Schardina* which is in the sea;" the personage representing this country is remarkable for his helmet, surmounted by a round ball; the Schardina are easily recognised as the ancestors of the Sardinians.—5°. "The chief of the enemies from *Schasou*;" the Schasou are well known in Egyptian history; they frequent that part of the desert which extends along the Egyptian frontiers by the Isthmus of Suez.—6°. "The country of *Toursa* which is in the sea;" these are the Tuscans or Etruscans.—7°. "The chief of the enemies from *Ka* . . .;" the mutilation which this portion of the precious list has undergone unfortunately precludes all possibility of identifying this people. The file of prisoners from Libya and from the Kousch country is even more mutilated; we may, however, still read :—1°. "The chief of the vile race of *Kousch;*" the artist has exceptionally given him the features of a negro, although Kousch was more accurately included by the Egyptians themselves in the Chamitic race.—2°. Destroyed.—3°. Also destroyed; the individual represented here was plainly a Kouschite.—4°. "The chief of the country of *Libou;*" his beard is pointed, and a lock of hair hangs over his ear. Here the identification is easy. These are evidently Libyans, the neighbours of the Egyptians on the western side.—5°. "The chief of the country of the *Toursas;*" another type of the Kouschites, whose aquiline nose and long fringed robe must not pass unnoticed.—6°. "The chief of the country of the *Maschaouasch*," so striking by the grandeur of his physiognomy. The Maschaouasch are the Μάξυες of Herodotus; they inhabited the northern coast of Africa, and constituted an important subdivision of Libya.—7°. "The chief of the country of the *Taraoua;*" this seventh personage completes, with the first, third and fifth, the series of the four Kouschite tribes who figure in this picture side by side with the Libyans.

In connection with the edifice to which this curious ethnographical series serves, so to speak, as an introduction, a question suggests itself which it will not be amiss briefly to discuss. Was the edifice which we have just entered really a palace? If so, this pavilion of Medinet--Abou is the only example of civil architecture which we possess. And yet, judging from this one specimen, we are led to assume that palaces were built of stone as solidly as the temples themselves. How is it then that we have no remains whatever of any other palace? We are not prepared to decide here the question as to where the kings had their abode, a question which has become more and more difficult to solve since we have ascertained that they did not inhabit the temples. We are, however, inclined to think that the founder of Medinet-Abou never intended to make this pavilion his dwelling-place. Its general architecture, as seen from afar amidst the landscape, recalls those triumphal towers (*migdol*) represented in the bas-reliefs of Karnak, of Luxor, of the Rameseum, and of Medinet-Abou itself, and which the kings of Egypt were wont to erect on their frontiers, at once as a means of defence, and as a memorial of their victories. The pavilion of Medinet-Abou might therefore be considered not as an example of civil architecture, but rather as a monument of military achievement, commemorative of a king pre-eminently warlike.*

B. The temple of Medinet-Abou was, like the palace, entirely constructed and decorated by Rameses III. The first pylon forms by itself a monograph which would afford interesting materials for special study. Large stelæ bearing date of the 11th and 12th years record the history

---

* It will be noticed that the summit of the encircling wall of the towers that form the main part of the palace is crenellated, which gives still more to the edifice the appearance of a fortification. The form of these Medinet-Abou battlements leads one to suppose that they may originally have been formed of the shields of soldiers thus disposed in rows, so as to be seen from the outside in time of peace, or to protect the warrior in the hour of battle. We should not venture upon this conjecture if a passage in Ezekiel (xxvii. 11), referring to bucklers suspended round the walls of Tyre, did not seem to afford some foundation to the idea.

of the glorious expeditions undertaken by Rameses against the Libyans, the Maschaouash, and other nations from the coasts of the Mediterranean who had leagued themselves together against Egypt. On the northern side of the façade of the pylon is a picture which deserves a special mention on account of the poetic turn imparted to one of its inscriptions. The king strikes with his falchion a group of kneeling prisoners. Ammon-Armachis presents him with the battle-axe. The deity addresses the king in a speech which we reproduce in the words of an excellent translation lately supplied by our friend M. Chabas:—

"My son, the fruit of my loins, thou whom I love, the lord over the two worlds, Rameses III., champion of the sword over the whole earth, the *Petti* of Nubia lie stretched out at thy feet.

" I bring thee the chiefs of the southern countries with their children on their backs, together with the precious produce of their lands. Spare the life of such as thou mayest choose amongst them; kill as many as it may seem good to thee.

" I turn my face to the north and I overwhelm thee with marvels. I bring *To-tescher* (the red land) under thy feet. Crush thy foolish enemies between thy fingers; overthrow the *Herouschaou* with thy victorious sword. I bring to thee also nations that know not Egypt, their coffers filled with gold, with silver, with pure lapis-lazuli, and all kinds of precious stones; the choicest products of *To-nuter* are before thy fair face.

" I turn my face to the east and I overwhelm thee with marvels. I unite them all together into thine hand; for thee I gather together all the produce of Pount; all the produce in *kami* and in precious *ana*, with every sort of odoriferous plants, is before thee.

" I turn myself to the west and I overwhelm thee with marvels. Ravage the country of the *Tahennou;* may they bow down before thee in adoration, or may they fall down as they fly from thy terrible voice."

In the court which immediately follows the first pylon, we find a remarkable instance of what Sir Gardner Wilkinson has ingeniously called the *symmetrophobia* of the Egyptians. This court is bounded on one side by large columns whose capitals represent the half-opened bud of the lotus; but on the other side, instead of similar columns we find massive stone pillars, to which are attached colossal statues of Rameses III. clothed with the attributes of Osiris.

On entering this court one faces the frontal of the second pylon. The southern pier is covered with a large picture. Ammon and Mout are on one side; on the other is Rameses bringing before the divinities a group of prisoners ranged in three rows. To judge by the general appearance of their costume, these prisoners must represent three branches of the same trunk. The lower group represents the *Poulista*, a people in whom M. Chabas recognises the Pelasgians, and who, according to another opinion, may be taken for Philistines, the ancestors of those who at a later period established themselves on the confines of Egypt. The middle group represents the *Tuanaouna*, who are the Daunians. Finally, in the upper group are the *Schakascha*, or Siculi, whose name is supplied by the inscription placed in front of the king. All these people, as we shall see, are inhabitants of the islands or of the shores of the Mediterranean, who had leagued themselves into a hostile confederation, and whom Rameses succeeded in conquering after brilliant encounters by land and by water.

On the northern pier is engraved a very long

and very precious inscription which has been ably interpreted by M. de Rougé. The first fifteen lines are little more than a tedious enumeration of the titles accorded to the king. The interest commences at the sixteenth line. Various nations of Asia, the people of *Kheta*, of *Kati*, of *Karkamaska*, of *Aratou*, and of *Arasa* were allied against Egypt. A second group, the *Poulista* (the Pelasgians), the *T''akkaraou* (the Teucrians), the *Schakascha* (the Siculi), the *Taanaouna* (the Daunians), the *Ouaschascha* (the Oscans), all maritime people, had joined the Asiatic nations. The encounter took place in a somewhat vaguely defined spot, possibly one of the mouths of the Nile. Victory crowned the efforts of Rameses, and Egypt once more escaped the danger of the terrible invasion with which she was threatened.

The granite doorway which unites the two piers of the second pylon is next passed, and a vast court is entered, which, taken as a whole, may be regarded as the most valuable relic that ancient Egypt has bequeathed to us. The court is completely surrounded by galleries covered with sculptures embellished with the most vivid colours. In front of the northern and southern galleries stand massive columns, their capitals representing the closed flower of the lotus. The eastern and western galleries were supported by square pillars, against which leant statues of the king. Roughly hewn shafts of sandstone columns encumber the centre of the court, while five of the same columns still remain upright. These are memorials of the time when, Medinet-Abou being a Coptic town, this magnificent court had been converted into a church. The pictures which cover the inner walls of the galleries are so numerous that it is impossible to describe them all. To the left on entering is a battle scene. The visitor must now be familiar with these gigantic figures of the king galloping in his chariot over enemies who fly in disorder. This time the enemies are the *Libou* (Libyans); low down in the picture, with a simplicity more surprising than pleasing, the artist has represented them tumbling one over the other. On the southern wall a second scene shows us Egyptian princes and generals leading prisoners before the victorious monarch. The prisoners, says an inscription, number one thousand, and there were three thousand slain. By the side is an inscription, unfortunately in a bad state of preservation, which refers to the same campaign.

In the third picture, the king returns to Egypt. He is preceded by several groups of prisoners in chains, and is accompanied by the troops. A fourth picture represents him entering Thebes and offering his prisoners to the gods of the city.

These large battle scenes occupy the whole of the lower register of the eastern, southern, and northern sides of the court. But on the upper register are represented scenes of a different character, which are no less worthy of attention. The illustrious founder of Egyptology describes them so well that we cannot do better than reproduce his words. "Rameses," says Champollion (*Lettres écrites d'Egypte*, p. 344 of the 1st edition), "quits his palace, carried in a richly decorated naos, or shrine, borne by twelve *œris* or military chiefs, whose heads are adorned with ostrich feathers. The monarch, decorated with all the marks of his sovereign power, is seated on an elegant throne, which golden images of truth and justice overshadow with their wings; the sphinx, emblem of wisdom combined with strength, and the lion, emblem of courage, stand near the throne, which they seem to protect. Officers wave around the naos the customary flabella and fans, young children of the sacerdotal caste march near the king, carrying his sceptre, the case for his bow, and his other insignia.

"Nine princes of the royal blood, high functionaries of the sacerdotal caste, and military chiefs follow the naos on foot, ranged in two lines. Warriors carry the pedestals and the steps of the naos. The procession is closed by a body of soldiers. Groups quite as varied precede the Pharaoh; a band of music, wherein may be distinguished the flute, the trumpet, the drum and chorus singers, forms the head of the procession; then come the relatives and favourites of the king, among whom may be noticed several high priests; and lastly, the eldest son of Rameses, second in command of the army, burns incense before his father's face.

" The king arrives at the temple of Horus, approaches the altar, pours out the libations and burns incense; twenty-two priests carry upon a rich palanquin the statue of the divinity, which advances surrounded by flabella and fans and flowering branches. The king, on foot, crowned with the simple diadem of the 'lower country,' precedes the god, and follows closely the white bull, the living symbol of Ammon-Horus or Ammon-Ra, his mother's consort. A priest waves incense before the sacred animal. The queen, the spouse of Rameses, witnesses all this religious pomp from an elevated position, and whilst one of the high priests reads aloud the prescribed invocation at the moment when the sacred light of the deity passes the threshold of his temple, nineteen priests advance, carrying on their shoulders the various sacred standards, the vases, tables of offerings and all the utensils belonging to the ceremonial; seven other priests lead on the religious procession bearing statuettes on their shoulders; these are the images of the royal ancestors and predecessors of Rameses, who thus participate in the triumph of their descendant."

Then comes the scene of the four birds, of which we curtail the description. The four birds are genii, children of Osiris and patrons of the four cardinal points. The high priest lets them fly, in order that they may proclaim to the south, to the north, to the west, and to the east, that, following the example of the god Horus, Rameses has crowned himself with the emblem of his dominion over the 'Upper and Lower Countries.' "The last part of the bas-relief," says Champollion, "represents the king, crowned with the *pschent*, giving thanks to the god in his temple.

The monarch, preceded by the entire sacerdotal body and by the sacred music, is attended by the officers of his household. He then cuts some ears of corn with a golden sickle and, wearing his military helmet as when he left his palace, pours out a libation and thus takes leave of the god Ammon-Horus, who has retired within his sanctuary. The queen is again witness of the two last ceremonies; the priest invokes the gods; a priestly scribe reads a long prayer; and the white bull and the images of the ancestral kings once more figure side by side with the Pharaoh."

The western side of the temple has been for some time the scene of considerable excavations, and some idea may be gathered of the enormous mass of rubbish that has been cleared away, from the fact that this point was the highest summit of the mound formed by the Coptic village above the temple. Unfortunately, the works have not produced the hoped-for results, as decapitated columns, empty chambers, and religious inscriptions of a trivial character are all that has been brought to light.*

* It was in the chamber of the north-west corner that, in raising the flagstones with which it is paved, nearly a thousand statuettes in bronze were found, all representing Osiris, and all more or less mutilated from the legs down-

The vast amount of historical facts which we have just been examining might lead one to imagine that all efforts were exhausted on the interior of the temple, and that Medinet-Abou could have very little more to show us. But this is far from being the case. A list of fêtes to be celebrated in the sacred edifice is engraved on the south side of the external wall. We will, however, pass this over in silence as it offers but little interest to such as do not wish to go deeply into the subject. But the north side of the external wall, half-buried though it be, is like a gallery in a museum. Ten pictures, symmetrically arranged, describe the incidents of a war undertaken by Rameses in the ninth year of his reign against the Libyans and the *T"akkaraou*.

1st picture.—Departure of the king and of the army; the soldiers are in marching order. The accoutrements of the troops should be studied.

2nd picture.—Grand battle and grand victory. The enemy are the Libyans of the race of the *Tamahou*. Like the heroes of Homer, the king is fighting in person, and the carnage is indescribable.

wards. This is but another proof that the custom prevailed of purifying the area of a temple by strewing it with divine images buried underground.

3rd picture.—12,535 of the enemy are killed; the generals bring the prisoners before the victorious king.

4th picture.—Harangue of the king to the general of the army. The troops are under arms, ready to march anew against the enemy. Many curious details.

5th picture.—Once more the troops are setting out and filing past. Here, as elsewhere, the texts consist of only a series of praises addressed to the king, and of thanksgivings to the gods.

6th picture.— Another battle and another victory. The enemies are the *T'akkaraou* whom the king overthrows. Women and children take flight in chariots drawn by oxen.

7th picture.—The march is renewed, and the enemy passes a country infested with lions, probably one of the fastnesses of Lebanon. The king has killed one lion and wounded another. It was probably somewhere about here that Amenophis III. killed the one hundred and ten lions, which, on a scarabœus in the Boolâk Museum, he boasts of having slain with his own hand during the first ten years of his reign.

8th picture.—Here we find the only representation which Egypt affords of a naval combat.

The scene is laid either close to the coast, or at the mouth of some river. The fleet of the *T'akkaraou*, reinforced by that of the *Schardina*, attacks the Egyptian ships. In the confusion that prevails, one of the enemy's vessels has sunk, and is seen floating keel upwards. Rameses stands on the shore, and his archers contribute to the victory of the Egyptian fleet by piercing the enemy with their darts.

9th picture.—The army sets out for Egypt, and stops at a fortified place called *Migdol-en--Rameses-hak-on*. The dead are counted by the number of hands cut off on the field of battle. A long file of prisoners passes before the king, who harangues his sons and his generals.

10th picture.—Triumphal return to Thebes. The king gives thanks to the gods. Speeches from the gods, speeches from the king, speeches even from the prisoners themselves who entreat the king to spare their lives that they may long celebrate his courage and valour.

This description of Medinet-Abou will suffice, we trust, to show the great importance of the admirable monument which we have just been studying in its most remarkable parts. If we now seek to realise the king's purpose in erecting it, the problem only admits of the same solution as in the case of the Rameseum. We may rest assured that the spot selected for its site, bordering at once on the desert and on the necropolis, was not idly chosen. We may read therein, as it were, an anxious thought for posterity and the founding of a sort of perpetual reminder of the illustrious dead. It is the memory of Rameses III., it is his very person that lives at Medinet-Abou.

THE NECROPOLIS.—The necropolis is reached from Luxor by the same route as the temples. The large square courts pierced on three sides with doors symmetrically disposed, which may be observed on the way to Goornah, are common tombs not worth noticing. But on leaving the temple of Goornah and following the border of cultivated land, one sees to the right some terraced hills in front of which the ground has been disturbed by innumerable excavations. This is the necropolis called *Drah-abou'l-Neggah*, undoubtedly the most ancient in Thebes. The tombs mostly date from the XIth and the XVIIth dynasties, and from the beginning of the XVIIIth. It was here that the kings Entef (XIth dynasty), whose mummy-cases are in Paris and in London, were found. Here also we discovered the sarcophagus of Queen Aah-Hotep, with its celebrated collection of jewels, now in the Boolák Museum. Unfortunately, there is not a single tomb in Drah-abou'l-Neggah which is worthy of a visit. The wealth and pomp of that period were all expended on the mummies; and external chapels, which moreover were of rare occurrence, bore no ornament whatever.

Further towards the south another part of the necropolis is reached, quite different in its aspect from Drah-abou'l-Neggah. This is *El--Assassif*. At Drah-abou'l-Neggah the earth disturbed by the excavation is yellow mingled with an inferior sort of broken brick, and it is only now and then that one comes upon a fragment of limestone. But at El-Assassif the soil consists, so to speak, of nothing but pounded limestone. This difference is accounted for partly by the fact that the rock out of which the tombs have been hollowed consists of a very fine white limestone, partly also by the customs of the period. Some of the tombs of El-Assassif belong to the XIXth and XXIInd dynasties, and especially to the XXXIst, and date therefore from a time when a greater amount of luxury was displayed in the ornamentation of the exterior chapels. In some places a few small edifices had been constructed which are unfortunately destroyed. On the other hand thick walls, also of limestone, which no doubt served to mark out the limits of the reserved portions of the necropolis, are frequently met with. All this has given to El-Assassif an aspect *sui generis* which Drah-abou'l-Neggah is far from possessing. We may add that the mummies are found here, not at the bottom of a deep well as at Sakkárah, but either simply in the earth itself, or in vaults constructed only a few feet below the surface. The tombs which can still be visited at El-Assassif, however, are neither numerous nor interesting. It would be impossible to describe their position without the help of a plan. The best way is to trust to the guides who are in the habit of showing them to travellers.

The two portions of the necropolis called respectively *Scheikh-abd-el-Goornah*, and *Goornat--Mouraï*, are found beyond that sort of circus of rocks of which El-Assassif occupies the centre. Here the tombs are hollowed out in the sides of the rocks themselves. Large square doorways open here and there upon the plain, and some of them are arranged in such regular order that seen from a distance they look like the batteries of a fortress. Moreover, an interest attaches to these tombs which those of El-Assassif and Drah--abou'l-Neggah do not possess. The arrangements are, generally speaking, on the same plan as at Sakkárah and Beni-Hassan. A chamber cut in the rock takes the place of the exterior chapel, where the survivors assemble to do honour to the defunct. A well opens out of that chamber, giving access to a mortuary vault closed to all eternity. The decorations afford in some instances materials of most interesting study, especially when episodes in the life of the defunct have furnished the subject. Thus the tomb of an individual called *Houï*, a functionary of the XVIIIth dynasty, contains some paintings which, unfortunately, are rapidly fading away, but which are none the less deserving of being studied. Houï, under the title of prince of Kousch, had been governor general of the Soudân, and one of the pictures represents him in the act of arriving to take possession of his government. People of every shade of complexion and of every race present themselves before him. Some are negroes with distinctive features strongly marked; others are of the negro type but brown in colour; others, also copper-coloured, have more northerly features; there are also men of a red tint like the Egyptians, mingled with white-complexioned women. Giraffes and oxen with long horns terminating in the form of human hands are brought before Houï, who also receives rings of gold, ingots of copper, skins of wild animals, long-handled fans and ostrich feathers. Another picture shows Houï returning from a mission into the country of the *Rotennou* (the Assyrians) and presenting to the king, seated on his throne, the ambassadors of that nation, whose dress consists of a large robe of gaudy colours rolled several times round their body. Of their slaves, naked to the waist, some are red, some white. All wear a pointed beard. The gifts which they bring to the king consist of horses, lions, ingots of precious metals, and vases of gold and silver curiously fashioned. This one example suffices to show the interest that attaches to the tombs of Scheikh-abd-el-Goornah and of Goornat-Mouraï, which are almost without exception monuments of the XVIIIth and XIXth dynasties.

The visit to the tombs of the southern hills

being over, we retrace our steps, and, bending slightly to the left, proceed to *Deir-el-Bahari*.

On our way, we cross diagonally the western extremity of El-Assassif. At the bottom of a sort of ravine, the guides point out the entrance to a large tomb, that of *Petamenophis;* but no one should venture to enter it who is likely to be incommoded by the overpowering odour of bats which it exhales. A little farther on, a sort of large gateway in crude bricks attracts attention by the singular disposition of the bricks in the archway.* It is difficult to master thoroughly the part of the necropolis to which this gateway belongs, because, plundered in turn by the dealers in antiquities and the owners of the adjacent limekilns, it has suffered more during the first half of the present century than during the two or three thousand previous years of its existence. All that we may venture to assert is, that in the western corner of El--Assassif the most ancient tombs belong probably to the XVIIIth dynasty, and the most modern

* The bricks are disposed transversely, as in the arches of the Holborn Viaduct, where this arrangement was supposed to constitute a novelty, as well as a marvel of engineering.

16*

may with some show of reason be assigned to the immediate successors of Alexander.

Deir-el-Bahari. — The temple of Deir-el--Bahari occupies the centre of the semicircle which encloses El-Assassif. It lies close against some fine perpendicular rocks, which, on the opposite or north-western side, run down into the valley of *Bab-el-Molouk*. There can be little doubt as to the origin of this temple. Deir-el--Bahari was raised to the glory of Queen Hatasou just as Medinet-Abou was raised to the glory of Rameses III. The site of these commemorative temples was chosen from religious motives peculiar to Egypt, to which there is no need again to allude. The walls of Deir-el-Bahari are covered with various cartouches which at first sight are calculated to cause a certain confusion in the visitor's mind. The fact is Hatasou took to herself different names according as she either shared the throne with her two brothers Thothmes II. and Thothmes III., or as she subsequently governed with the title of Regent in the name of the latter of these two princes, or again, as she eventually reigned alone in her own name. Science has not yet, we think, said its last word on the subject of these different names, and perhaps the solution of the problem may be found in some inscriptions lately brought to light in the temple we are now examining.

Deir-el-Bahari was constructed on a singular plan, and even from a distance it bears no resemblance to any of the other temples of Egypt. It was preceded by a long alley of sphinxes, now utterly destroyed, and by two obelisks of which nothing at present remains but the base. Beyond these, it stretched out in terraces as far as the mountain, one court leading up to another by easy ascents. It was built of a fine white limestone, and one might well wonder that a single block of wall should remain standing, if one did not remember that El-Assassif, by the abundance of its materials and its proximity to the plain, offered to the enterprising plunderer much greater facilities of spoil than could be obtained at Deir--el-Bahari. Moreover, it is probable that this temple was soon abandoned. Even as early as the XXIInd dynasty it was already used as a cemetery, and in one of its chambers were found, piled up one above the other almost to the ceiling, mummies of the Grecian period, lying over rows of other mummies, of which the most ancient probably belonged to the XXVIth dynasty.

History is not forgotten at Deir-el-Bahari, any more than at the Rameseum and at Medinet--Abou. But it is no easy matter to determine whether the fragments of pictures one meets with scattered here and there form part of any one common theme. Reaching the temple from the east, that is nearly at its lowest part, we come upon the first of these bas-reliefs. Troops are marching, preceded by trumpets and officers; the soldiers are fully equipped, some carrying in their hands branches of palm trees; their standards are surmounted by the cartouches of Hatasou. Evidently we have before our eyes the triumphal entry of troops returning from a campaign. Further on, almost at the extremity of the temple, and only a few steps from the granite gateway which forms so conspicuous an object from all parts of the surrounding plain, is another picture somewhat more distinct; but unfortunately the final portion only remains, Hatasou had sent her troops on a campaign into Arabia, a country celebrated for its perfumes, its spice-bearing and odoriferous trees, its gold, its ebony, and its wrought fabrics of every sort. The expedition was to lay in a stock of such treasures as it could collect together, and to bring them back to Thebes to be stored in the temple of Ammon. No obstacle, it would seem, checked the progress of the detachment sent for this purpose to the shores of the Red Sea. The principal inhabitants of the country embarked more or less willingly on the Egyptian fleet to lay at the feet of the magnificent Regent substantial proofs of their submission. Such are the principal episodes of that campaign as described in the bas-reliefs of Deir-el-Bahari. The scene is laid on the sea-shore, the transparency of the water naïvely allowing the fishes to be perceived. Some Egyptian soldiers are drawn up on the coast. The inhabitants of the Pount country quit their dwellings, whose white roofs have the form of a cupola, and bring the produce of the soil and of their industry. Some are piling up the scented gum into enormous heaps, others bring entire trees, the roots of which are tied up in *couffes* or frail baskets. The clothing of these individuals, their weapons, and the colour of their skins, deserve especial study. The Egyptian fleet is drawn up close by, and the loading of the ships is proceeded with. Bales of goods, earthen jars, live animals, trees—everything is carefully arranged in its appointed place. The ships are propelled both by sail and by oars. Thebes at last is reached, and the different items are enumerated. There is quite a procession of cynocephalous monkeys, panthers, giraffes, and short-horned oxen; while collars, chains, bracelets, daggers and hatchets, are all being classed in order. Ammon is witness of the scene, and addresses his congratulations to the Queen Regent. In a side chamber to the south, another subject is presented. We have now no longer the green waters of the Red Sea, but the blue waters of the Nile. In the lowest compartment of the picture, more troops are seen marching. But, interesting as they are, one cannot be sure whether these episodes refer to the same campaign which has been so minutely described on the walls of the principal chamber. Close by, a fine doorway, with many ruins heaped up before it, leads into a chamber, the colours of which have retained all their vividness. On each side of the passage leading to this chamber, an admirable sculpture represents a royal personage, who quenches his thirst with the milk of Hathor under the form of the most beautiful cow that the Egyptian bas-reliefs can show us.

BAB-EL-MOLOUK.—Bab-el-Molouk is the St. Denis of the kings of the XIXth and the XXth dynasties. A bifurcation of the road leads into another valley situated a little further to the west, where the last kings of the XVIIIth dynasty are interred. The former only of these two valleys is usually visited, being the burial place of the kings of the XIXth and XXth dynasties. The path which leads to it may, indeed, be called the path of the dead. Not a blade of grass is to be seen; all is sad and gloomy as if burnt up with some internal fire which has split and blackened the rocks. The distance from the banks of the Nile is nearly four miles.

The "Tombs of the Kings" at Bab-el-Molouk are all excavated out of the solid rock, and consist of inclined passages which penetrate more or less deeply into the mountain itself. When once the royal mummy had been deposited in its resting-place, the entrance was walled up, and the surrounding rock was levelled so as to leave no external trace of the situation of the tomb. This shows that the spirit in which these royal monuments were erected is totally different from that which regulated the construction of all other tombs. In the case of these royal sepultures, the ordinary external chamber where the survivors assembled to do honour to the memory of the dead were represented by the large commemorative edifices erected at the entrance of the necropolis. Of these the most important, being solidly constructed, have alone stood the test of ages. The number of tombs open in the principal valley, up to the year 1835, was twenty-one; during our explorations the number has reached twenty-five, but they are not all kings' tombs. Princes and even functionaries of a high rank were admitted to the honour of seeing their tombs excavated by the side of those of the sovereigns of their country. "Above the *Memnonium*," says Strabo, "are some tombs of kings cut in the rock in the form of grottoes, about forty in number, admirably wrought, and well worthy of a visit." On the face of this passage, it was surmised that well-directed excavations in Bab-el-Molouk might lead to the discovery of the fifteen missing tombs. But it may be that Strabo included in his reckoning the tombs of the Valley of the Queens. Be that as it may, from Amenophis III., with whom the series begins (as the first kings of the XVIIIth dynasty are not at Bab-el-Molouk), down to the last king of the XXth dynasty, there is no prince of any note missing except Horus. Now, as Horus is the last sovereign of the XVIIIth dynasty, his tomb is more likely to be found in the Valley of the West, and we are strongly inclined to think that excavations, however vigorously carried on at Bab-el-Molouk, would not be rewarded by results commensurate with the labour which the remoteness of the spot and the difficulty of supplying the workmen with water must necessarily entail. The Valley of the West is alone worth exploring, pick-axe in hand; for the kings of the XVIIIth dynasty whose tombs are yet unknown might be discovered there.

Such travellers as do not make archæology their special study may content themselves with visiting the four following " Tombs of the Kings " :—

1°. *Tomb of Sethi I.*, commonly called *Belzoni's Tomb*. This is the most magnificent of all the Tombs of Bab-el-Molouk; by its grandeur and the profusion of sculptures with which it is adorned, it eclipses all others. It was discovered in 1817 by Belzoni. It had already been violated, but still not a single bas-relief was then missing from its walls, and its pictures yet retained their original freshness. The visitor, however, will soon perceive to what sad mutilations it has since been subjected. Rumour attributes these acts of vandalism to certain explorers of Egypt who must, however, be above the reach of such suspicion by virtue of the very services they have rendered to Egyptology. It is more correct to say that that desecration of one of the most valuable monuments of Egypt is the work of dealers in antiquities, or even of the tourists themselves. The fact is that the latter in their recklessness purchase almost at any price relics which, after all, are simply the proceeds of an irreparable wrong done to science.

Immediately on entering the tomb, the visitor finds himself actually transported into a new world. The almost joyous pictures of the Sakḳárah and Beni-Hassan tombs have altogether disappeared. The defunct is no more to be seen at home, in the midst of his family. No more making of furniture; no more building of ships; no more extensive farm-yards, with cattle, oxen, antelopes, wild goats, geese, ducks, demoiselle cranes, marching in procession before the stewards. All has become, so to speak, fantastic and chimerical. Even the gods themselves assume strange forms. Long serpents glide hither and thither round the rooms, or stand erect against the doorways. Some convicted malefactors are being decapitated and others are precipitated into the flames. Well might a visitor feel a kind of horror creeping over him if he did not realise that after all, underneath all these strange representations lies the most consoling of all dogmas, that which vouchsafes eternal happiness to the soul after the many trials of this life. Such in fact is the meaning of the pictures which adorn the walls of this tomb. It has been said that before according to their kings the honours of burial, the Egyptians passed judgment upon them. This legend must of course be understood in an allegorical sense. The judgment of the soul after being separated from the body, and the many trials which it will be called upon to overcome by the aid only of such virtues as it has evinced while on earth, constitute the subject-matter of the almost endless representations which cover the tomb, from the entrance to the extreme end of the last chamber. The serpents standing erect over each portal, darting out venom, are the guardians of the gates of heaven—the soul cannot pass unless justified by works of piety and benevolence. The long texts displayed over other parts of the walls are magnificent hymns to which the soul gives utterance in honour of the divinity whose glory and greatness it thus celebrates. When once the dead has been adjudged worthy of life eternal, these ordeals are at an end; he becomes part of the divine essence, and, henceforward a pure spirit, he wanders over the vast regions where the stars for ever shine. Thus the tomb is only the emblem of the voyage of the soul to its eternal abode. The soul has no sooner left the body than we are called upon from room to room to witness its progress as it appears before the gods and becomes gradually purified, until at last in the grand hall at the end of the tomb we are present at its final admission into that life " which a second death shall never reach."

When Belzoni discovered the tomb, a fine sarcophagus in alabaster stood in the furthest chamber, but this was subsequently carried away to England, and is now in Sir John Soane's Museum. In the centre of this same chamber is a passage which penetrates some distance into the ground. The tomb was to have extended further in that direction, but whether Sethi died before it could be finished, or whether, as was more probably the case, a layer of argillaceous marl was encountered which offered serious obstacles to further progress, this passage was discontinued, and its entrance out of the chamber was hidden by a paving stone over which the sarcophagus was finally deposited.

2°. *Tomb of Rameses III.*, commonly called *Bruce's Tomb*, or the *Tomb of the Harpists*. If Sethi's tomb is remarkable for the perfection of its sculptures and the beauty of the models which it affords to the student of art, that of Rameses III., on the contrary, is mean, and unworthy of the hero of Medinet-Abou, and yet the nature of the subjects is extremely interesting. Towards the middle of the tomb and on either side of the two first passages are some chambers which merit attention. The most varied scenes, with boats, household furniture and utensils, coats of arms, bows, arrows, and pikes, are represented here. One of these pictures, treated with a breadth of style not to be found in the other parts of the tomb, is that of the celebrated harpists, already so well known by the many copies which have been made of them. The name of *Bruce's Tomb* was given to the tomb of Rameses III. in memory of the traveller of that name who was the first to visit it and to make it known to the world.

On entering the tomb it soon becomes apparent that the original plan was departed from, and that the entrance passage instead of continuing in a straight line suddenly bears to the right. This is owing to the carelessness with which the Egyptians excavated their tombs. The architect entrusted with the piercing of the tomb of Rameses had in fact taken his measure so badly that a few yards from the entrance he stumbled upon an adjoining tomb which he was obliged to avoid by modifying his original design.

In the principal chamber of the tomb formerly existed a sarcophagus in pink granite, cut in the form of a royal cartouche. This was carried away by Mr. Salt; the lower part is at the Louvre and the cover is at Cambridge, in the Fitzwilliam Museum.

Many Greek *graffiti* are found in the tomb of Rameses III. This feature, however, is not peculiar to the subterranean tomb we are now considering. Many other sepulchres are covered with similar inscriptions, and often in still greater numbers. This shows that the tombs of Bab-el--Molouk were visited by strangers even as far back as the times of the Ptolemies; these, however, could only be the tombs of which the royal mummies had already been violated and dispersed by Cambyses, a circumstance which, in the eyes of the Egyptian, entirely took away the sacred character of these monuments.

3°. *Tomb of Sethi II.* This tomb, which is situated at the extreme end of the valley to the west, possesses nothing worthy of attention except some pictures clumsily sculptured in relief which are seen to the right and to the left on entering. The eye which has grown accustomed to the delicacy of the sculptures of the tomb of Sethi I. will not easily become reconciled to the roundness of style of these sculptures, however attractive they may appear at first sight.

4°. *Tomb of Rameses IV.* This differs from the others by its width, the high pitch of its roof, and the very slight inclination of its floor; it might be visited, so to speak, on horseback. At the end, lies the granite sarcophagus of gigantic proportions. The insipid paintings of this tomb, however, and its lifeless sculptures can hardly prove of much interest after Belzoni's tomb, especially as they are covered with a mass of Greek *graffiti* which make them still more indistinct.

To such travellers as are not already satisfied with the inspection of the four grand tombs we have just described we would point out the *Tomb of Rameses VI.*, which, judging by the testimony of the *graffiti* found in the interior, was, for some unknown reason, designated by the ancients the *Tomb of Memnon*. It is remarkable for the astronomical representations on its ceiling. The tomb of Rameses IX. also possesses a certain interest. The amount of time which the artists must have spent in the decoration of the walls is something appalling. In the strange pictures where the principle of generation plays so large a part one should only see a forcible and energetic application of those ideas of resurrection after death and of the immortality promised to the deceased which pervade this tomb. The tomb of Rameses VI. is the N° 9 of Wilkinson; that of Rameses IX. is called N° 6; and it is under these numbers that they are usually pointed out to travellers by the guides.

There are three routes to choose from in

leaving Bab-el-Molouk. Tourists who have but little time to spare will return by the way they came, that route being the most direct. If time permit, the path which ascends the mountain may be taken; and the summit once reached, the descent, which is rather steep and available only for pedestrians, may be made either to the east or to the south. The former path leads by Deir-el-Bahari to El Assassif; the latter, after a rather long *détour*, comes out behind Medinet--Abou, and thus affords the opportunity of revisiting that temple, as well as the Rameseum and the temple of Goornah.

V.—ESNEH.

	Miles
From Luxor to Erment	9
,, Erment to Esneh	27
From Luxor to Esneh	36

From Boolák to Esneh, 500 miles.

The temple of Esneh is situated in the middle of the town. The only part that is now visible is the hypostyl hall which has been cleared out to the pavement. It is said that other parts of the temple still exist almost intact under the houses in the town which effectually conceal them from view. According to another account,

Champollion himself visited the sanctuary where he recognised the name of Thothmes III. ; but these statements are not sufficiently authenticated. Be that as it may, the large portico or entrance-hall supported by columns is all that is now to be seen of the temple of Esneh.

The façade and columns of this portico are of the Roman epoch. Here one meets with the cartouches of Claudius, Domitian, Commodus, Septimius Severus, Caracalla and Geta. Further in the style is Grecian and can be traced to Ptolemy Philometor. The sculptures in this temple are of the very worst execution, and the inscriptions are so spoiled with the forced meanings of letters, with puns and *double entendre*, that it requires a very close attention and special aptitude to guess the exact sense which lies hidden under these wretched hieroglyphs. And yet the capitals of columns, through their coat of black smoke, show a careful and delicate workmanship and a purity of form which at first sight one is surprised to meet with in a temple of this period. The fact is, architecture did not follow engraving and sculpture in their rapid downfall. Indeed, whilst almost from the advent of the Ptolemies engraving and sculpture had begun to decline, as if the Greeks could not accommodate themselves to the conventionalities and somewhat unnatural forms with which tradition had trammelled both arts, architecture, on the contrary, received a fresh impetus and gained materially in freedom of style. Although the principle of monolithic architraves was not to be given up at once, so as to allow of the space between the columns being widened, yet the column itself became more graceful and rose more boldly to the ceiling; and it was especially in the decoration of the capitals that the improvement was felt. Doubtless the lovely group of full-blown lotus of which the capitals of the columns at Philæ, for instance, afford such striking examples, is already in bud at Medinet--Abou and at Karnak. But these ancient forms were modified and modernised under the Greeks, and new ones created. In short, the Greeks allowed the grand traditional art of sculpture in relief to perish in their hands, almost from their arrival in Egypt; but, on the other hand, architecture, being less hieratic in its character, took a fresh start from that same period; for it was only under the Greek dynasties that a form of column began to appear which no longer seemed crushed under its architraves, together with that form of capital with curiously interlaced lines of which the pronaos at Esneh offers some remarkable specimens.

VI.—EDFOU.

	Miles
From Esneh to El-Kab	20
,, El-Kab to Edfou	12
From Esneh to Edfou	32

From Boolák to Edfou, 532 miles.

Between Esneh and Edfou the only spot worth stopping at is El-Kab, the ancient Eileithyias, or the "city of Lucina"—a place famous for its grottoes and for a very small temple of the XVIIIth dynasty, built in the plain, about two miles away from the river. This was formerly a strategical point, being situated at the entrance of the mountain-gorge down which the *Herouscha* (the Bisharees of the present day) were enabled to make frequent inroads into the Egyptian territory, as recorded in the inscriptions of the time. A fortress had therefore been erected here, and its ramparts may still be seen. It was built of crude bricks, and probably dated from the ancient empire.

The Temple of Edfou is one of those monuments which speak for themselves, and to which no description can do justice. Its magnificent pylon and encircling wall are unique in Egypt. As for the temple itself, no one can fail to be struck with its close resemblance to that of Denderah in its general plan, if not in its architectural details. The excavation of Edfou is the most extensive archæological work ever executed under the auspices of H.H. the Khedive. A few years ago, the modern village had invaded the temple, its very terraces being covered over with dwellings, stables, and storehouses of every kind. In the interior the chambers were filled with rubbish almost to the ceiling. The amount of time and trouble expended on the excavations will be realised on entering the temple, where every single line of inscriptions has now become perfectly accessible to the traveller and the antiquarian.

The Temple of Edfou was founded by Ptolemy IV. Philopator, who constructed the sanctuary as well as the surrounding chambers, the chapel, and, generally speaking, the whole of the furthermost part of the temple properly so called. The decoration of some of the inner chambers was the work of Ptolemy VI. Philometor. The hypostyl hall, which forms a sort of monumental frontage to the edifice, was constructed by Philometor and Ptolemy IX Euergetes II. The outer passage bears on one side the names of the same Euergetes, and on the other those of Ptolemy XI Alexander; lastly, the pylon was decorated, if not actually constructed, under the reign of Ptolemy XIII Dionysos.

Some curious inscriptions, which cover a portion of the sub-basement, deserve notice. They inform us that each chamber had its name, so that nothing would be easier than to draw up in hieroglyphs the topographical plan of the edifice. The dimensions of all the chambers are also given in cubits and in subdivisions of cubits, and as we are able to refer to the chambers themselves, we thus possess an exact and valuable standard of comparison between the ancient and modern Egyptian measures. Moreover, the architect of the temple, whose name was *Ei-em-hotep Oer--si-Phtah* (*Imouthes*, the great son of *Phtah*) has put his name to his work. Nor must we omit to mention that another inscription tells us that the temple, begun under Philopator, finished under Euergetes II., was completed, after interruptions caused by wars, in ninety-five years; which statement doubtless applies to the actual construction only, and not to the decoration, since from the beginning of the reign of Philopator to the death of Dionysos, the last of the kings whose cartouches appear on the temple, no less than 170 years elapsed.

In a corner of one of the chambers, where it has most probably been thrust by comparatively modern hands, is a monolith of fine speckled gray granite which deservedly attracts attention. At Denderah the *sanctum sanctorum* is a niche in the wall of one of the chambers at the extreme end of the temple. Here the most holy place is represented by the monument we are now considering. The inscriptions with which it is covered certify both as to its date and as to the spot from which it was originally hewn; and we may take it for granted that this very monolith was hollowed out by Nectanebo I. (XXXth dynasty) to serve as the naos or shrine of a temple now destroyed and which was replaced by the present edifice. We need not add that this massive sort of shrine served here, as at Denderah, to enclose the mysterious emblem which was the tutelary deity of the temple.

The temple of Edfou, exclusive of the pylon

and the encircling wall, has a frontage of forty metres, or 131 English feet 3 inches, and a total depth of 71 metres 85 c., or 236 English feet. Including the pylon, its façade measures 249ft. 10in., and its depth 451ft. 6in. The height of the pylon is 114ft. 10in., being 32ft. 10in. less than the Vendome column.

It is so evident that the temples of Edfou and Denderah were constructed on the same plan, and sprang up from the same train of thought, answering to the same religious requirements, that the practical use to which certain portions were put must have been the same in one temple as in the other. The study of the inscriptions at Edfou leaves no doubt as to this point. The priests assembled in the second hall of columns; the grand procession of New Year's day was prepared within the chapel, the offerings were stored up in certain chambers, &c. As for the pylon, nothing indicates that it was ever used for any other purpose than to signal from afar the edifice to which it served as an ornamental gateway. On the external frontage of the pylon are four prism-shaped cavities which are vertical at the bottom. The purpose of these is manifest. It was into these cavities that the enormous masts were fitted in, whose long pennants contributed to the decoration of the pylon. These masts must have been nearly 150 feet in height, and could never have been sufficiently secure had they not been supported against the pylon by some suitable apparatus; it was as receptacles for this apparatus and to give it fair play that those inner chambers of the pylon were used, the square windows of which may be seen from the exterior in the vertical lines of the grooves.

VII.—GEBEL-SILSILEH.

	Miles
From Edfou to Gebel-Silsileh	$26\frac{1}{2}$
,, Boolák to Gebel-Silsileh	$558\frac{1}{2}$

Owing to the excellence of the sandstone, the proximity of the stream on either side, and the facilities of landing afforded to heavily laden boats, the spot we have now reached has long been the centre of the most extensive stone works which exist in Egypt.

The most remarkable quarries of Gebel-Silsileh are on the right bank of the river, and are mostly open to the sky. Some are cut in sharp edges to the height of fifty or sixty feet, others are arranged in tiers of huge receding steps. The methodical care, however, we had almost said the extreme caution, with which the stone has been quarried, is remarkable throughout. It would seem as though the mountain had been cut into blocks with as much regularity as planks would be cut by a skilful carpenter from the trunk of some valuable tree. Were we not already convinced of the fact, a visit to Gebel-Silsileh would prove that the explosive force of gunpowder was unknown to those by whom these quarries were worked.

The quarries on the left bank are neither so extensive nor so easy of access. But the existence at the very edge of the stream of a certain number of grottoes invests them with an interest which the others do not possess. Of these grottoes some are mere ordinary tombs. The most numerous are due to the custom which prevailed among the Egyptians to leave a proscynem, a stela, or a monument of some sort, as a record of their visit to certain spots considered holy. Thus at Gebel-Silsileh, where the Nile, which is here shut in between two mountains, was the object of a special worship, we find, engraved on the rock, hymns addressed to the river by no means wanting in a certain loftiness of style. The type of these commemorative monuments is the large speos, conspicuous from a distance by its four massive pillars. It dates from the reign of Horus, the last king of the XVIIIth dynasty, but was made use of later on by many personages who have left here valuable records of their passage. Our limits will not allow of our attempting to describe all that is interesting in this speos. We will only refer to the two pictures which are sculptured side by side in the south-west angle.

The one on the southern wall represents a goddess nourishing King Horus, still an infant, with her divine milk. Egypt, it is true, never attained to the ideal of the beautiful as did Greece, nor indeed is it probable that she ever made the attempt. But, taken as a specimen of Egyptian art, the bas-relief of the speos of Gebel-Silsileh is a most beautiful work. Nowhere can greater purity of outline be found; and this picture is marked by a placid sweetness of expression which excites at once wonder and admiration. Close by, on the western wall, is the other picture well known under the title of the *Triumph of Horus*. The king is seated on his throne, borne by twelve officers of his army; two other warriors hold over his head a long-handled flabellum.

This is the triumphal return into Egypt after a victorious expedition against the Kouschites of the Soudan. Armed soldiers lead the procession, followed by terror-stricken prisoners.

VIII.—ASSOUĀN.

	Miles
From Gebel-Silsileh to Ombos	15
,, Ombos to Assouān	$27\frac{1}{2}$
From Gebel-Silsileh to Assouān ...	$42\frac{1}{2}$

From Boolák to Assouān 601 miles.

Ombos is passed on the way from Gebel-Silsileh. There is hardly anything to be said about this monument, which sooner or later is doomed to become the prey of the Nile, however carefully it may be protected. The work of Grecian princes, the successors of Alexander, like Edfou and Denderah, it bears in several places the names of Philometor, of Euergetes II., and of Dionysos. It presents the peculiar feature of consisting to a certain extent of two temples placed in juxtaposition, dedicated to the two eternally antagonistic principles—that is, on the one hand, light adored under the name of Horus; on the other, darkness symbolised by the crocodile-god Sebek.

If Ombos were to be visited with the intention

only of finding out its date, it would scarcely be necessary to land. The very first glimpse one obtains of the temple marks it out as of Ptolemaïc origin. The ideas suggested by the temple of Esneh are in fact reproduced here. With the arrival of the Greeks, Egyptian architecture received an impetus which gave birth to the column with a capital *sui generis* found only on temples of Greco-Egyptian origin.

The distance between Ombos and Assouān is not great. After a few hours' journey, one begins to perceive towards the south mountains apparently crowned with forts. At their feet lies an island of vivid green dividing the stream into two almost equal parts. To the left a few white houses in the midst of an oasis of date-palms faintly light up the landscape. But what chiefly characterises the approach to Assouān is that the river seems to end here, and the eye seeks in vain for some outlet.

Assouān always takes the traveller by surprise. One seems to be quite in a new world —Egypt finishes and another country begins. Nowhere does one find such a motley crowd of Egyptians, Turks, Barabras, half-naked Bisharees and negroes of every tribe. The inhabitants of Khartoom especially are remarkable by their grand mien, their black skin and their finely formed head that reminds one of the best types of northern races. To complete the picture, on the shore may be seen merchandise, gums, elephants' tusks, and skins of animals, in outlandish-looking packages which add to the bewilderment of the traveller. In the midst of the crowd circulate hawkers, no longer trading in antiquities, but in bludgeons of ebony, pikes, lances and arrows the iron points of which are said to be poisoned. Assouän has scarcely retained any vestiges of the past, but there are many points of interest in the town. A little away to the south, in a hollow of the ground, lies a small temple of Ptolemaïc origin lately discovered. About half a mile further on, is an obelisk still adhering by one of its sides to the quarry out of which it had begun to be hewn.

On the western side of the river immediately opposite to Assouän is the island of Elephantine. Whilst at Assouän the Egyptian element still predominates in the population, at Elephantine the traveller finds himself entirely surrounded by Nubians. At the beginning of the century a temple might still be seen at Elephantine, already in ruins, which was called by the authors of the great work of the Egyptian Commission the Northern Temple. There was also a temple of admirable proportions called the Southern Temple, and, judging by the drawings made at that time, it must have been built by Amenophis III. Assouān boasted besides of a monumental gateway of granite, and a quay rising abruptly from the river flanked on the northern side by a nilometer. In 1822, both temples as well as the nilometer disappeared. The quay of Roman workmanship, for which many remains of still more ancient edifices were utilised, is still standing, as also the granite portal which bears on each of its uprights the cartouches of Amenophis II. Close to the modern dwellings, an indifferent statue of Osiris, on which may with difficulty be deciphered the names of Menephtah (XIXth dynasty, 1350 B.C.), marks the spot where once stood the façade of the temple of Amenophis III.

IX.—PHILÆ.

	Miles
From Assouān to Philæ	5
,, Boolák to Philæ	606

The excursion from Assouān to Philæ may be made by land as far as the convent of the

Austrian Mission, from whence travellers are conveyed to the island in boats. But a branch of the same road leading to the village of Shellâl, where boats may also be had, will be found far more picturesque, when the condition of the river makes it practicable.

From Philæ back to Assouān a different route is generally followed, in order to enable the traveller to visit the so-called cataract.*

From Assouān to the convent of the Austrian Mission the journey lies the whole way through the desert. Here we find ourselves surrounded by a granite formation which crops out above the surface of the ground on all sides; and this granite heaped up into gloomy masses gives a peculiarly desolate appearance to the landscape.

* Paul Lucas, a traveller of the time of Louis XIV., described the cataract as precipitating itself with such force from the top of the rocks that the inhabitants of the district were deaf for several miles around. Now this is a manifest exaggeration. Indeed, if by cataract we are to understand the fall of water caused by the sudden lowering of the entire bed of the stream, as for instance in the case of the Rhine at Schaffhausen, it may certainly be said that there exists no cataract at Assouān. True, when the Nile is low, the rocks with which its bed is obstructed project out of the water and small falls are thus produced, which in some places swell into cascades. But when the river is high these cascades are considerably reduced, and the rock being almost entirely covered they dwindle down into mere rapids.

In describing Gebel-Silsileh we alluded to the custom which prevailed among the Egyptians of recording their passage through certain places by a stela or an inscription. Of this we have innumerable instances along the route from Assouan to Philæ—inscriptions on the rocks abound on all sides. Sometimes they consist merely of proper names, but more often they assume the proportions of a tableau. The passer-by has represented himself as adoring the gods of the cataract; underneath is the inevitable form of prayer. On more memorable occasions we read of generals, princes, and even kings returning from an expedition into Soudán who have left on the rock by the wayside a lasting record of their passage. It is easy to realise what valuable data may occasionally be supplied by these memorials, which bear more upon history than on religion. Schayl, a small island in the cataract, not always easily accessible, is, so to speak, covered with such records, some of which have yielded a clue to historical facts now universally accepted.

The history of Philæ is soon told. Its most ancient monuments precede only by a few years the time of Alexander, as no name occurs here of an earlier date than that of Nectanebo II. This monarch it was who raised the little temple situated to the extreme south of the island, and of which only a dozen columns now remain; he also it was who erected the large portal placed between the piers of the first pylon. We will not weary the reader with the enumeration of all the Ptolemies and Cæsars who subsequently erected numerous edifices over the island. Numbers of Greek laudatory inscriptions, especially on the first pylon, have been left by pilgrims visiting the shrine; and from two of these proscynems we gather this important fact, that, so late as A.D. 453, under the Emperor Marcian—*i.e.*, about seventy-four years after the edict of Theodosius had abolished the Egyptian religion—there still lived in the "Holy Island" priestly families who continued to celebrate the time-honoured mysteries of Osiris and Isis.

But perhaps in a spot unequalled throughout Egypt in beauty it would be too much to expect of the visitor that he should examine closely into the origin of the monuments. In fact, at Philæ, as at Karnak, the impression of the moment must prevail over the memories evoked, and no one can help being fascinated by the picturesque beauty and striking grandeur of the landscape, with the sombre rocks that frown on all sides, and the cataract that roars in the distance. On the other hand, the effect produced on the mind by the first view of the lovely columns of the little temple commonly known as *Pharaoh's Bed* defies all attempts at description. Nor is that first impression otherwise than fully confirmed by a stroll through the island; and one feels that such a spot is the most fitting crowning point to the voyage in Upper Egypt.

www.ingramcontent.com/pod-product-compliance
Lightning Source LLC
Chambersburg PA
CBHW031928230426
43672CB00010B/1854